Free Trade vs. Tariffs: A Reasoned ⌐

An anti-tariff cartoon from 1880s

The harder the consumer is hit, the higher the profits for corporations.

Rev. 02/12/2026

Feedback: alsnewideas@gmail.com

Other books by Alan Sewell   https://www.amazon.com/Alan-Sewell/e/B00557PQDY

Contents

Preface

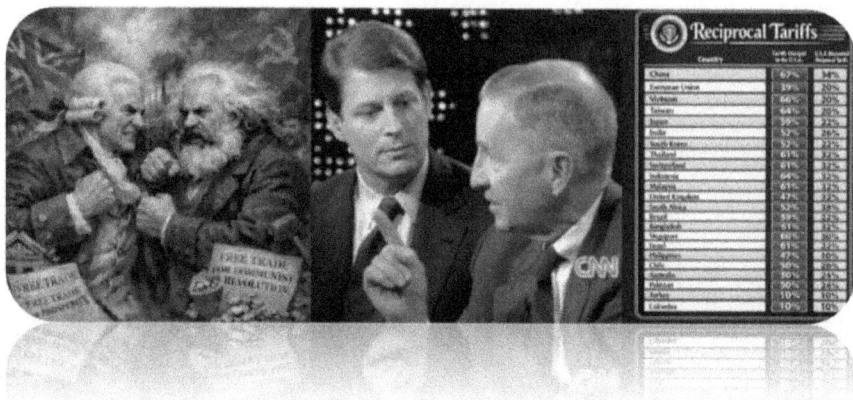

Ten months have passed since April 2, 2025, designated "Liberation Day" by President Trump, when he announced several classes of tariffs on most products imported from most countries. He then reduced the tariffs, claiming their leaders agreed to allow greater access to their markets for U.S. products and to invest $trillions in moving production to the United States.

As of early February 2026, Trump's tariffs are in the following classes:

- Product-specific tariffs applied to most countries of 25% on motor vehicles and 50% on steel and aluminum, including the steel and aluminum in manufactured products, for example, the steel and aluminum in cans, appliances, etc.

- Tariffs of 10% to 15% on countries we have reasonably balanced trade with, but higher with a few countries where trade is chronically unbalanced.

- Our USMCA partners Canada and Mexico are exempt from tariffs on most products with at least 75% value created in the three countries. However, motor vehicles, steel, and aluminum are tariffed exceptions as is the value of aluminum or steel content in any product imported from Canada and Mexico. Also, a few perennially tariffed products like softwood imports from Canada, having nothing to do with Trump's tariffs.

- Higher tariffs on many products of Chinese manufacture, where the trade imbalance severe. Cumulatively, tariffs on Chinese product average around 30%.

- The *Di Minimis* exemption of tariffs on imported items shipped in packages declared less than $800 in value was repealed. The value of foreign-sourced packages of any value is now tariffed.

- Policy tariffs, such as 50% levied on Brazil for alleged political oppression and 50% on India for buying Russian oil, reduced to 18% in early February when India's government said they had stopped buying Russian oil.

Trump's tariffs are estimated, when December's numbers are reported to complete the year, to reduce the trade deficit with China from $295 billion in 2024 to $206 billion in 2025, a decrease from the peak of $418 billion in 2018 when Trump's first term tariffs were declared. Production of imports bound for the United States has been relocated from China to Vietnam and Mexico, prospering those countries, and some production returned to the United States. The tariff revenue averaged $33 billion a month in the last months of 2025. Contrary to expectations of the friends of free trade, who expected a reincarnation of the Smoot Hawley tariffs of 1930, the economy grew at 4.6% in the last reported quarter for 2025 and inflation cooled to 2.7%, while the DOW soared to a record 50,000. The headline on February 11, 2026 is *US job growth accelerates in January, unemployment rate falls to 4.3%,* good for workers, and disappointing the foes of tariffs who hoped for a bad news comeuppance for President Trump. But Trump's onerous way of imposing tariffs has driven our relations with our most important trading and geopolitical ally Canada to their lowest point since the War of 1812, instigating a bipartisan rebellion in Congress to eliminate them. Tariff foes are furious with the flippant way Trump imposes them, draws them down, then threatens to impose them again.

The primary question is whether the tariffs have achieved their intended purpose of reshoring industry to the United States, and if so, whether they have inflicted disproportionate damage on other sectors of the economy. An even more fundamental question is whether they comply with the Constitution's designation of Congress as the taxing authority. This book is purposed to provide information on both sides of these questions. If I sometimes poke fun at the dogma of unconditional "Free Trade Mavens," it is nevertheless with respect for the authority the friends of free trade have garnered since the days of Adam Smith.

Tariffs are a historical and practical interest of mine, as an author of books on economic history and a developer of international trade management software that calculated tariffs on U.S. exports to Canada, the European Union, South America, and Asian countries. I believe trade is unquestionably beneficial between countries in a true common market whereby companies in any country produce for the combined market of both, and there are no anti-competitive factors, such as one country's government restricting the importation of the other country's products.

I am skeptical of chronic trade deficits with countries that are primarily labor substitution markets to replace American workers in the manufacture of products exported to the USA. To me, this kind of trade recalls the discredited Luddite theory of employing multitudes of cheap laborers instead of investing in improving worker productivity here. I believe it diminishes innovation in the USA while paying foreign workers too little to engage in reciprocal trade of buying American-made products. But I understand the counter-argument that suggests we are increasing our standard of living by importing more products than we could produce with American labor.

I wonder if trading away our people's livelihoods for marginally cheaper imported goods is on balance beneficial to our people, our social cohesion, and our national security. Most economists theorize that trade, even if disruptive of some workers' livelihoods in the short term, channels the economy into the most productive pursuits by forcing people and businesses to upgrade their productivity in creating goods and services that have the highest value for the long term. But is there a point where too much disruption in too short a time becomes detrimental short term and long term?

My fundamental principle of evaluating trade is whether it is reciprocal. If it is reasonably well balanced between the trading partners, it is probably fair. If it is severely imbalanced, with one partner going deeper into debt to pay for imports, while exporting jobs and wealth to trade surplus countries, then I believe trade may require tariffs to balance it. I believe tariffs are a fair way to balance trade with countries that practice unfair trade practices by deceptive ruses such as claiming that one country's products do not comply with another country's commercial laws.

I understand the libertarian position that "trade is transactions between individuals, not governments, so individuals should be able to buy whatever they want, from wherever they want, without the government imposing tariffs on foreign goods." But there is a countervailing principle that markets are a public, as well as private, interest, and that individuals are never allowed to buy whatever they want from wherever they want. A city government does not allow unlicensed vendors to set up shop anywhere they want to sell whatever they want, even if townspeople want to buy it, because the established businesses that invest in the community, who hire people in the community, and who pay taxes in the community, have created a presence in the community that should, within reason, be protected from cutthroat itinerant competition, selling merchandise of dubious origin, especially if some of it is burglarized from the next town.

I also understand the propensity of the friends of free trade to engage in mindless platitudes like, "I run a trade deficit with my grocery store." Everybody except the grocer runs a deficit with the grocery store. But a prudent person does not mortgage a paid-off house to run a trade deficit with everybody.

I understand the arguments for and against tariffs from these multiple perspectives and seek to bring a broad discussion to the tariff controversy. It is a vexing question now and has been since our founding. Like the wise President Lincoln, I do not know if we will ever "mature our judgment" on this complex subject of conflicting interests, but I will try to give a fair hearing to all points of view. I am a popular blogger and reviewer of books on economics:

- *Alan, We can always count on you for a cogent, sober analysis. Bravo and thanks again*
- *Of all commenters I look forward to seeing yours. Erudite, cogent, and relevant, and informative. Thanks.*
- *Alan, I agree and want to thank you, personally, as well. I thank you for your remarkable commentary supported by hard facts. You have changed my mind about some things through the excellence of your arguments, always*

supported by hard facts and documentation. You are an asset beyond compare to this community. Thank you so very much.

- *Mr. Sewell has made me rethink a number of ideas I thought were set in historical concrete.*
- *Your advice could not have been more eloquently phrased had Winston Churchill been your editor.*
- *Once again, thank you, Alan Sewell. You are one of the most insightful and rational Americans in existence.*

A Steady and Persistent Agitation

An anti-tariff cartoon from 1880s

The harder the consumer is hit, the higher the profits for corporations.

As with all general propositions, doubtless, there will be shades of difference in construing this. I have by no means a thoroughly matured judgment upon this subject, especially as to details; some general ideas are about all. – President Abraham Lincoln, speaking on the tariff question.

The question of free trade vs. tariffs is back on the front burner of public policy with the return of Donald Trump to the White House. During his first term, he imposed tariffs on imports of steel and washing machines and put broad tariffs of 35% on many products from China. He ended negotiations to join the Trans-Pacific Partnership. He reincarnated NAFTA as the USMCA to favor trade with Mexico and

Canada over countries in Europe and Asia by raising the North American content rule from 62.5% to 75% and requiring automakers in Mexico that export cars to the United States to pay some Mexican workers a minimum wage of $16 / hour to lessen their labor differential with American workers.

He was elected again by larger popular and electoral vote margins after vociferously promising broader tariffs --- claiming "tariff is the most beautiful word in the dictionary." He enacted tariffs as the common denominator of international trade instead of the exception, including with Canada and Mexico, rekindling the eternal debate between free traders and trade managers. These controversies are as old as the United States. As Senator, Secretary of State, and presidential Candidate James G. Blaine wrote in his book *Twenty Years of Congress* in 1884:

Public attention may be temporarily engrossed by some exigent subject of controversy, but the tariff alone steadily and persistently recurs for agitation, and for what is termed settlement. Thus far in our history, settlement has only been the basis of new agitation, and each successive agitation leads again to new settlement.

The industrial classes study the question closely; and, in many of the manufacturing establishments of the country, the man who is working for day wages will be found as keenly alive to the effect of a change in the protective duty as the stockholder whose dividends are to be affected. Thus, capital and labor coalesce in favor of high duties to protect the manufacturer, and, united, they form a political force which has been engaged in an economic battle from the foundation of the government. Sometimes they have suffered signal defeat, and sometimes they have gained signal victories.

11

Another 140 years have passed and the Free Trade vs. Tariffs debate continues as steadily and persistently as ever. It provokes "eternal agitation" because it concerns a broad spectrum of economic, political, and ideological belief. Free trade champions see trade creating a bright, modern, wealthy, well-informed and peaceable world, whereas they see tariffs as creating a world inefficient, poor, parochial, and prone to war.

Even trade skeptics acknowledge its benefits in a reciprocal common market where no country seeks to advantage itself with protectionism; and where the differences in wages are not excessive, such that companies in some countries profit by replacing their workers with foreign labor earning less. But they rebuke trade with countries that don't trade reciprocally as a deliberate national policy. They lament the thousand miles of de-industrialized wreck and ruin across America's formerly prosperous Industrial States, stretching from Pennsylvania to eastern Iowa, leaving behind an economically debilitated population suffering premature deaths from despair.

Truth and hyperbole color both views. We should seek a perspective approximate with reality, so we may discern circumstances where trade should be constrained by high tariffs, or whether low revenue tariffs are a necessary response to other country's VATs on our trade. I advocate free trade where I believe on balance it benefits Americans, while favoring tariffs where I believe trade is detrimental and uncorrectable by any other means.

I learned the mechanics of tariffs by developing information systems to manage international trade in the USA, Canada, Europe, Asia, and South America. I've lived, worked, and owned businesses in some of those countries. I've written about the history of tariffs and their impact on the United States at various stages of our economic development. I seek to invoke a reasoned understanding of the *Free Trade vs. Tariffs* debate by exploring its historical roots and evolution to the present; analyzing the differences of opinion between free traders and those who believe there are circumstances where trade should be restricted. Because this is an issue of political ideology as well as economics, opinions become vociferous when tariffs are discussed.

"Tariffs create trade wars where everybody loses," say those who favor free trade in all circumstances, including with countries that do not trade reciprocally with us.

"Tariffs are taxes on consumers!" say many Conservatives. Even Liberals, who advocate raising every other tax on Americans, resist tariffs. Whenever tariffs are discussed, these tax-happy people become the greatest tax protestors since Lady Godiva rode naked through town on a horse.

Libertarians say the government must not impose tariffs to restrict their freedom to purchase whatever they want from wherever they want. If they can buy products of superior value from any foreign country, then that is where they want to buy them. They say this promotes economic efficiency and a proper allocation of our labor and capital to those things we do better than other countries. Let the other countries supply what we consume, if they can do it at higher quality and/or lower cost than we can. If our companies and workers can't compete, let them perish. But hopefully, the stress of competition will induce them to move into higher value occupations and add more value to our economy than what we are handing off to foreigners.

Trade skeptics may reply that life does not always work in this happy way, when millions of people are simultaneously unemployed by imports, and many will never recover the livelihoods trade ended. They say production comes prior to, and is preeminent over consumption, because people and nations cannot indefinitely consume more than they produce, unless they go into debt by mortgaging paid off assets. As our trade deficit has ballooned, so has our national debt, because trade deficit dollars do not always return to the United States, and when they do, are not always invested constructively. Although the trade deficit and the national debt are two different things, they move in tandem, because U.S. Treasury debt must be issued to buy imports in excess of what we export.

Free Traders may respond, "As long as the economy is growing faster than the national debt, we should keep buying merchandise where it is cheapest, because when we save money buying from other countries, we may invest the savings in more productive enterprises that grow our wealth."

Free trade skeptics may counter, "How many times have we heard people claim they can afford to keep buying more than they produce by loading up on debt, and then the debt spiral bankrupts them? Many nations, once wealthy and now poor, lost their ability to produce because they thought they could exchange their previously acquired wealth for goods produced by other countries. Then there's the question of whether people would rather have jobs enabling them to buy domestic products, even if they are relatively expensive, than to be unemployed by imports and unable to buy anything, even if it is relatively cheap."

They point out that industrial traditions lost to other countries cannot be recovered, resulting in the debilitation of a nation's knowledge to create wealth in the future, as well as a loss of present wealth. Furthermore, people do not always buy imports by choice; they buy them because companies stock their shelves with imports that inflate their profit margins. And further, that some American companies move production overseas because profits earned overseas are not taxed by the United States. American companies can produce in overseas tax havens, sell the products in the United States without paying taxes to the United States, and repatriate their overseas profits to the United States tax free. Whereas American companies that produce in the United States are taxed copiously.

These points, counterpoints, and counter-counterpoints follow each other endlessly in the carousel of debate. Perspectives differ, depending on whether one's livelihood relies more on production or consumption. This book seeks to explain the perspectives so we can properly decide whether to support unconditional free trade, or to favor tariffs on trade in some circumstances.

The premise of this book is that free trade may be presumed beneficial between countries of similar cultures, legal systems, and standards of living that want common markets of production and consumption such as we have between the USA and Canada. But we must be wary of trade with countries purposed as labor substitution markets that do not buy reciprocally from us. And with countries like those in the European Union having free trade among themselves, while erecting trade barriers to avoid buying reciprocally from us. And especially with countries like China that engage in cyberattacks and theft of intellectual property while using trade to extract wealth from other countries rather than as a mutually beneficial exchange of goods and services.

Adam Smith vs. Karl Marx

The debate over Free Trade vs. Tariffs usually ends with appeals to the authority figures of Adam Smith, David Ricardo, and Milton Friedman. Many free trade acolytes paraphrase what they think these authority figures wrote without ever having read them. Adam Smith, the presumed father of free trade, wrote like a labor union leader:

No society can surely be flourishing and happy, of which the far greater part of the members are poor and miserable. It is but equity, besides, that they who feed, clothe, and lodge the whole body of the people, should have such a share of the produce of their own labor as to be themselves tolerably well fed, clothed, and lodged.

The progressive state is, in reality, the cheerful and the hearty state to all the different orders of the society; the stationary is dull; the declining melancholy. The liberal reward of labor, as it encourages the propagation, so it increases the industry of the common people.

The wages of labor are the encouragement of industry, which, like every other human quality, improves in proportion to the encouragement it receives. A plentiful subsistence increases the bodily strength of the laborer, and the comfortable hope of bettering his condition, and of ending his days, perhaps, in ease and plenty, animates him to exert that strength to the utmost.

Where wages are high, accordingly, we shall always find the workmen more active, diligent, and expeditious, than where they are low.

Smith, Adam (2013-09-12). The Wealth of Nations (Illustrated) (p. 31) Kindle Edition.

He favored trade that raised employment and wages but not trade that destroys workers' livelihoods by importing from countries where labor is cheaper. He recognized that a nation's wealth derives mostly from industry:

The most opulent nations, indeed, generally excel all their neighbors in agriculture as well as in manufactures; but they are commonly more distinguished by their superiority in the latter than in the former.

Smith, Adam. The Wealth of Nations (Illustrated)

Karl Marx, the father of communism, favored free trade because he believed it incited desperate unemployed workers into riot and revolution:

But, generally speaking, the Protective system these days is conservative, while the Free Trade system works destructively. It breaks up old nationalities and carries antagonism of proletariat and bourgeoisie to the uttermost point. In a word, the Free Trade system hastens the Social Revolution. In this revolutionary sense alone, gentlemen, I am in favor of Free Trade.

As Marx predicted, our politics has become extreme in an era of abundant free trade, as competition from a global labor pool drives down wages of the working class, while inflating the value of the stocks, bonds, and real estate of the investing classes. As these words are written, the morning headline on CNN is lamenting Trump's recent election:

https://www.cnn.com/2025/02/06/politics/trump-power-grabs-analysis/index.html

Millions of Americans voted for a candidate who argued that the federal government was not responding to their needs – after a grueling chapter of history marked by financial crises, the hollowing out of the manufacturing base, foreign wars and punishingly high inflation.

This book is not about politics, because both parties have factions that favor free trade in all circumstances and those who favor tariffs in some circumstances. President Biden, a Democrat, not only maintained and expanded the tariffs imposed by President Trump, the Republican Populist, but also imposed a 100% tariff of his own on Chinese EVs. Many in both parties strenuously object to the tariffs. The book is more about the question CNN raised: Why did we endure so much economic hardship in the 2000s, leading to the election of tariff-prone presidents and the unravelling of the Globalist system of governance, anchored around international trade?

Free Trade

Adam Smith peruses a tariff schedule

To the friends of free trade, "tariff" conjures up trade follies of Medieval European towns imposing tariffs on products from surrounding towns. And our infamous Smoot-Hawley tariff of 1930 that many economists say slowed economic recovery during the Great Depression, while provoking authoritarian rulers of Germany, Italy, and Japan to attempt to conquer economically self-sufficient autarchy areas by invading nearby countries and brutalizing their people. Tariffs are the bane of free market champions going back to Adam Smith's *The Wealth of Nations* coincidentally published in 1776 when tariffs and other oppressions of Britain's government were igniting our American Revolution.

Smith's premise is that free trade raises standards of living by improving efficiencies in consumption and production. When a product is sold in a large market, there are more consumers to spread overhead costs of running the business over, so prices will be lower, if the usual market forces of supply and demand are present. On the production side, he says, "The division of labor is limited by the extent of the market." He means that a larger market has not only more consumers, but also more productive workers with more differentiated skills. Larger markets create more competition, more efficiency, more profits for business, and higher wages for workers.

Besides economic efficiency, trade binds businesses, governments, and people of different nations together, thereby fostering peaceable relations and making wars fought for the conquest of markets and natural resources unthinkable. Trade promotes economic and political freedom whereby countries with business-friendly governments are usually more productive than countries with oppressive governments harassing businesses and individuals with taxes, regulations, and political conformity edicts.

The ideological foundation for free trade is the freedom to choose, according to the fathers of libertarian economics from David Ricardo and Adam Smith to Milton Friedman. People should be able to buy and sell, within reason, wherever they want. There is also anti-tax, anti-regulation, and limited government ideology among Libertarians who believe our government will be forced to lower taxes and decrease regulations to remain competitive in a world of free trade.

Free Trade as a Founding Principle

The United States was founded on a tradition of free trade that makes us historically skeptical of tariffs. American Colonists on the Atlantic Seaboard were a seafaring people, accustomed to trading with European nations. Even at that early date China, Japan, and other Asian countries beckoned as the prizes of overseas trade. We wanted to trade with other countries on our own terms, without having Britain's government impose tariffs on our imports and excise taxes on our exports to enrich their treasury at our expense.

The European powers were staking claims to China, India, Africa, the Middle East, and the Caribbean. These empires conquered by the British, French, Dutch, Spanish, and Portuguese became monopolistic trading zones, only open to trade between the colonies and the home countries. Their colonial peoples were designated "hewers of wood and drawers of water" who enriched the colonial powers by providing them with cheap-labor production of raw materials, and a captive market for the manufactured products of the colonial powers' homeland sold at monopoly prices.

Our first armed conflicts after the Revolutionary War were fought to secure access to foreign markets. These were the Barbary (Shores of Tripoli) War of 1801-1805, the Quasi-War with France in 1798-1800, and the War of 1812 with Britain. These were primarily naval conflicts designed to suppress state-sponsored piracy in the Mediterranean, and to vindicate our right to trade with warring British, French, and neutral European countries. We also took early steps to prevent the European powers from re-establishing their empires in the Western Hemisphere. President James Monroe declared in 1823 that any European nation attempting to establish a new colony in the

Western Hemisphere risked war with the United States; the Western Hemisphere must remain open to trade with the United States.

To facilitate trade with Asia, Americans were settling Hawaii in the early 1800s, about the same time as our first pioneers reached the banks of the Mississippi River. In 1853 Senator William Seward, who later became President Lincoln's Secretary of State, advised Americans to:

"Open up a highway from New York to San Francisco. Put your domain under cultivation and your ten thousand wheels of manufacture in motion. Multiply your ships and send them forth to the East (Japan, China, and India). The nation that draws the most materials and provisions from the earth, and fabricates the most, and sells the most of production and fabrics to foreign nations, must be, and will be, the great power of the earth."

As our economy shifted from farming to industrial employment, our economic cycles of boom and bust intensified. The economy grew rapidly after the Civil War, but the growth was too erratic to maintain stable employment. The economy fell into a series of depressions with high unemployment and social disturbances that required the military occupation of major cities to prevent mobs of unemployed hungry workers from looting and burning them. In 1877 unemployed workers in St. Louis, attempting to establish a workers' commune, were defeated by the U.S. Army. These disturbances increased during the severe depression of 1894-1898 when Chicago, the rail hub of the nation, was placed under military occupation, and the U.S. Army shot down rioting railroad workers, driven to desperation by layoffs and wage cuts, to get the trains moving. President Gover Cleveland's Secretary of State Walter Gresham remarked:

"We cannot afford constant employment for our labor. Our mills and factories can supply the demand by running seven or eight months out of twelve. There is undoubtedly an element of danger in the present condition of society.... I am not a pessimist, but what is transpiring in Pennsylvania, Ohio, Indiana, and Illinois, and in regions west of there may fairly be viewed as symptoms of revolution.

Other economists and newspapers described the economic devastation of 1894-1898.

- *The American people are in the throes of a fiasco unprecedented even in their broad experience. Ruin and disaster run riot over the land.*
- *The panic of last year is nothing compared with the reign of terror that exists in the large centers. Business is at a standstill and the people are becoming thoroughly*

aroused. Their feeling is finding expression about as it did during the War of the Rebellion.

- *Hard times are with us. The country is distracted; very few things are marketable at a price above the cost of production; tens of thousands are out of employment; hungered and half-starved men are banding into armies and marching toward Washington; the cry of distress is heard on every hand; business is paralyzed; commerce is at a standstill; riots and strikes prevail through the land,*
- *The United States is dangerously near the conditions of things at the time of the French Revolution.*
- *The nation is fighting for its own existence just as truly as in suppressing the Great Rebellion [Civil War].*

Our business and political leaders believed that exporting our surplus productions to Asia's large populations of Asia would keep our workers employed:

- *The increase of home consumption did not keep pace with the increase of forth-putting and facility of distribution offered by steam. Whether they will or no, Americans must now begin to look outward. The growing production of the country demands it. An increasing volume of public sentiment demands it.*
- *It behooves us to accept the commanding position the United States has among the powers of the earth. This country was once the pioneer and is now the millionaire. What is the present crying need of our commercial interests? It is more markets and larger markets for the consumption and products of the industry and inventive genius of the American people.*

- *Future historians will call the events of 1898 the turning point of American history. The change was inevitable, had long been preparing, and could not have been long delayed. The American people had begun to realize that their industrial and commercial development should not be checked by the limitation of the demands of the home market, but must be furthered by free access to all markets; that to secure such access the nation must be formidable not merely in its wants and wishes and latent capabilities but in the means at hand wherewith to readily exert and enforce them.*

Our great leap across the Pacific occurred when we went to war with Spain in 1898. The war was ostensibly about liberating Cuba from Spain's oppressive colonialism. However, we sent our new Asiatic Fleet, with an invasion army in tow, 7,000 miles across the Pacific, in the opposite direction of Cuba, to "liberate" Spain's Philippine Islands colony and repurposes it as a naval base to protect our access to Asian markets. Hawaii became a Territory of the United States in 1998. It, along with Guam and American Samoa, became the coaling stations and naval bases to link our West Coast to the Philippine Territory, our perch in the heart of Asia to ensure our trading rights were not infringed.

Our interest in maintaining trade with China ignited our entry into World War II when Japan attacked our military bases at Pearl Harbor and the Philippines after we demanded they cease and desist from their conquest of China. Imperial Japan was in league with Hitler's Nazi Germany and Mussolini's Fascist Italy, their common denominator of aggression being the conquest of imperial domains they could exploit by enslaving or killing the native populations and seizing their land, farms, and natural resources, especially oil and industrial minerals. President Franklin Roosevelt and our Congress authorized our supply of weapons to Britain, the Soviet Union fighting Nazi Germany and Fascist Italy, as well and the Chinese factions fighting the Japanese, thereby involving us in the European War to destroy the genocidal regimes of Hitler and Mussolini, as well as the Japanese Imperialists.

Emerging victorious in World War II, we made free trade a foundation of peace and prosperity for the post-war world. We granted free access to our markets to our allies and defeated enemies. We

26

declared our dollar convertible to gold at $35 / ounce so all nations could settle their trades in a currency that could not be devalued. We established trade-promoting agreements and organizations such as the General Agreement on Tariffs and Trade (GATT), the World Trade Organization, and The World Bank.

Although our historical political tradition is that Democrats are free traders and Republicans protectionists, that difference disappeared in 1940 when the Republicans nominated Wendell Wilke as their presidential candidate, author of *One World* proposing a post-war World Government to guarantee free trade among all nations. The United States did implement its spirit of trade by opening our market to imports from all nations while not requiring them to buy reciprocally from us. Until Trump, Ronald Reagan was the only Republican President whose administration had a protectionist hue, his tariffs purposed as temporary restraints on imports to buy time for U.S. companies to retool for improved competitive efficiency.

The effects of international trade were beneficial perhaps even beyond expectations. The demolished nations of Western Europe were rebuilt. Communists in France, Germany, Italy, and Greece, were made irrelevant by the return of prosperity. Incipient Communists in burned-out Japan faded away. The prosperity of the United States and our global allies, united by trade, eventually convinced the Soviet Union and China to adopt forms of state-sponsored capitalism. The Soviet Union dissolved, while China reached approximate economic parity with the United States, albeit by using the United States as a one-way market to sell to, without buying reciprocally from us. Although Russia and China remain authoritarian states, they became less virulent when sterile communism yielded to capitalist prosperity.

We entered the 21st Century with a justifiable faith in trade as an engine of prosperity and democracy. We believe free trade is a foreign policy as well as economic interest. We believe it decreases the propensity of foreign governments to attempt to increase their wealth by conquering other countries. We believe it destabilizes authoritarian regimes by bringing their people into contact with us and exposing them to our values of democracy and human rights. We believe it encourages all nations to join with us in a prosperous global trading community, as political allies, and friends with common values of human rights and democracy. When the new Millennium arrived at midnight 2000, President Bill Clinton anticipated a new century of peace, progress, and prosperity:

We are fortunate to be alive at this moment in history. Never before has our nation enjoyed, at once, so much prosperity and social progress with so little internal crisis and so few external threats My fellow Americans, we have crossed the bridge to the twenty-first century.

Our Trade Agreements

Any country's government may unilaterally open its market to tariff-free imports from any or all countries. If a government wants to obtain reciprocal access to other countries' markets, a free trade agreement is necessary.

The United States has free trade with twenty countries, starting with Canada and Mexico and including Australia, Bahrain, Chile, Colombia, Costa Rica, Dominican Republic, El Salvador, Guatemala, Honduras, Israel, Jordan, South Korea, Morocco, Nicaragua, Oman, Panama, Peru, and Singapore. I often hear people say we should have free trade with some of these countries, like Australia, not knowing we've had it for decades.

These agreements approximate free trade because they have loopholes allowing protection of industries deemed essential for economic and political stability. For example, even with the USMCA, the United States is not permitted to supply more than 3% of Canada's dairy products market, considered a national unity issue due to the concentration of dairy farms in secession-prone Quebec. The United States likewise protects some products from Canadian competition; for example, by raising the tariff on Canadian softwood from 8% to 14% in 2024. I will therefore use the term "free trade" to describe trade mostly, but not entirely, unobstructed by tariffs or unreasonable government regulations designed to stifle imports.

Free trade treaties are most likely to be mutually beneficial between kindred countries with similar laws and living standards, i.e. the countries of the European Union or between the United States and Canada. These trade treaties are purposed to create **common markets** whereby goods and services produced in any country compete on equal terms with all other member countries' goods and services. American companies don't move production to Canada to hire cheap labor to build product exported to the United States. Nor do Canadian companies move production to the USA to export to Canada. Aside from the minor protectionism of lumber and dairy products, and the recent impositions of President Trump, the USA and Canada are a true common market with balanced trade fostering common prosperity for workers, consumers, and corporations.

A close approximation of free trade is the General Agree on Tariffs and Trade (GATT), signed by every significant country It seeks to limit tariffs to a maximum of 2.5% on manufactured products and 5% on farm produce. Every significant country has signed onto GATT, so in theory every country has free trade with every other country, or at least a close approximation to it via GATT. However, most countries signed GATT with the expectation of freely exporting to other countries, while protecting the home market against competing imports.

Free Trade Reconsidered

When the harmonious adjustment of international trade shall ultimately be established by the Parliament of man in the Federation of the world, the power of production and the power of consumption will properly balance each other; but in traversing the long road and enduring the painful process by which that end shall be reached, the protectionist claims that his theory of revenue preserves the newer nations from being devoured by the older, and offers to human labor a shield against the exactions of capital.

So wrote Republican Senator, Secretary of State, and presidential candidate James Blaine in 1884. We still don't have "a Parliament of man in the Federation of the World" to assure free trade with production and consumption in balance everywhere to offer "human labor a shield against the exactions of capital." The closest we have come is the continent-wide national market inside the United States and the common market with free movement of people and businesses inside the European Union; albeit the E.U. was diminished when the United Kingdom left in 2016, the year Donald Trump was elected to rein in detrimental trade and immigration here. The proposed Trans-Pacific Partnership was also rejected and there is some sentiment in the USA and Canada to eject Mexico from NAFTA / USMCA.

The primary objection to trade is its propensity to destroy employment in developed countries by substituting cheaper labor from poorer countries. This is a sort of reverse colonialism where trade destroys employment and wages in the developed countries that used to own colonies as captive markets to dump the home country's surplus production. Blaine continued:

Free-traders do not, and apparently dare not, face the plain truth—which is that the lowest priced fabric means the lowest priced labor...[they] have at times attempted to deny the truth of the statement; but every impartial investigation thus far has conclusively proved that labor is better paid, and the average condition of the laboring man more comfortable, in the United States than in any European country.

Blaine was a capitalist speaking as a friend of labor, the way Adam Smith did, because wise business owners know they will not prosper unless their laborers are paid enough to purchase the products their labor produces. Another trade problem Blaine mentioned, then as now, is the governments of some countries subsidizing their industries to keep them producing more than the home market requires so they can dump their surplus production at a loss in other countries, thereby keeping people in the home country employed while putting workers in the dumped-upon countries out of employment.

Deciding whether to protect the livelihoods of workers vs. keeping the country open to the lowest-cost imports, even if produced with cheap labor or foreign government subsidies, is a difficult question in boisterous democracies like the United States. Our Democratic Party has traditionally represented itself as a friend of people of modest means, including factory workers as well as consumers. Because every person is a consumer, but not everyone is a factory worker, the Democrats have been the party of free trade. Presidents Bill Clinton and Barak Obama, and presidential candidate Hillary Clinton, backed NAFTA and the Trans-Pacific Partnership, knowing it would harm their labor union voters, but believing free trade was in the best interests of the 85% of American consumers who don't work factory jobs, as well as beneficial to the owners and investors of the 85% of business enterprises in the USA that are not industrial companies.

The Republican Party has traditionally prioritized the interests of business owners and investors, making Republicans amenable to protecting with tariffs the capital invested in industrial companies. There are not enough business owners to win elections, so Republicans knew they had to appeal to factory workers. When the Republican Party has represented itself as the friend of labor, it has gained authority and popularity in the public mind far beyond what is possible for any party representing only the interests of capital. They did so magnificently, winning the votes of most industrial workers in the pivotal election of 1896, thereby dominating national politics until 1932, excepting 1912 to 1920 when the party split. Republican Presidents Nixon and Reagan were elected by appealing to industrial workers, Reagan helping them and their employers by levying more tariffs on imports than any president since Herbert Hoover. Trump was elected on the same promise of tariffs in 2016 and 2024, as a steelworker in Latrobe, Pennsylvania said at a rally days before the 2024 election:

The president has saved the steel industry. You saved it with tariffs. You're my hero and the greatest president ever. We want to endorse you and give you a hard hat.

In 2024 My Florida Senator Marco Rubio, soon to become Trump's Secretary of State, concurred:

Even elites, though, can't outrun the costs of their decisions forever. Decades of deindustrialization have made America dependent on the nation's chief adversary, Communist China, for everything from the ingredients of our medicines to the inputs for our weapons systems.

Meanwhile, the relentless exportation of blue-collar jobs and importation of cheap labor have left countless US-born men without dignified work, sapping their opportunity and their strength—and no society can long thrive without strong men.

Time is running out to chart a new course. We must abandon the post-Cold War consensus, break multinational corporations' tariff taboo, reinvest in domestic production, and—crucially—regain control of our borders. In short, we must put the interests of our nation before the interests of our elites.

The longer we fail to do so, the greater a disservice we will do to the American citizenry: the very people who voted us into office and, in doing so, entrusted their welfare to our hands.

Free Trade: Hypothesis vs. Reality

President William McKinley of 1897-1901, known both for implementing tariffs and expanding U.S. markets overseas, spoke eloquently of the merits for trade:

The quest for trade is an incentive to human activity... to men of business to devise, invent, improve, and economize in the course of production. Business life, whether among ourselves or with other people, is ever a sharp struggle for success...The wisdom and energy of all the nations are none too great for the world's work.

Isolation is no longer possible or desirable. No nation can longer be indifferent to any other... Only a broad and enlightened policy will keep what we have.

He wanted trade that did not interrupt our home production or diminish the demand for labor:

By the sensible trade arrangement which will not interrupt our home production, we shall extend the outlets for our increasing surplus...What we produce beyond our domestic consumption must have a vent abroad. The excess must be relieved through a foreign outlet, and we should sell everywhere we can and buy wherever the buying will enlarge our sales and productions and thereby make a greater demand for home labor.

Reciprocity treaties are in harmony with the spirit of the times; measures of retaliation [tariffs] are not. If, perchance, some of our tariffs are no longer needed for revenue or to encourage and protect our industries at home, why should they not be employed to extend and promote our markets abroad?

...By the sensible trade arrangement which will not interrupt our home production...

This is always the dilemma with trade. Every nation wants trade that allows it to export its surplus productions, while accepting only those imports that do not harm its industries and workers. Nations want to participate in the bright world of trade outside the windows without letting it darken the rooms inside the house:

_https://www.huffingtonpost.com/ian-fletcher/how-do-other-nations-bala_b_628157.html_

How Do Other Nations Balance Their Trade? Try Germany

Germany, like the U.S., is nominally a free-trading country. The difference is that while the U.S. genuinely believes in free trade, Germany quietly follows a contrary [protectionist] tradition that goes back to the 19th-century German economist Friedrich List.... So, despite Germany's nominal policy of free trade, in reality, a huge key to its trading success is a vast and half-hidden thicket of de facto non-tariff trade barriers.

Germany is the core of the European Union, a trade cartel that promotes trade with its members by excluding competing imports from the United States:

Example: EU has a 29% tax (10% tariff and a 19% import VAT) on all American made cars. Their claim that they charge an average of 3% is statistically true but a lie, because that average is not in actual trade dollars, but across all product categories (definitions,) many of which the USA does not export into EU. The 3% average gives American car imports as exactly the statistical weight as non-existent American Penguin imports. They have very high tariffs that target American products that *compete with their domestic producers. Their tariff on American potato: 0%. Their tariff on American headphones: 42%.*

There are also informal trade barriers. You cannot sell American Wine in France for fear of getting your shop burned down. The core EU airlines refuse to buy Boeing airplanes. To understand these trade barriers, go to EU and you'll find that only American products available are ones that do not compete against EU products.

Countries like Japan and those in the European Union organize their economies along principles of "Democratic Socialism." In Germany, workers councils hold seats on each company's boards of directors and do not permit companies to move work overseas in search of cheap labor. The European Union is a trading club for its members. Nobody needs to put it in writing that purchases from outside the club, including imports from the United States, are discouraged. Japan, South Korea, and other Asian democracies are institutionalized cartels where manufacturers, distributors, retailers, and banks have common ownership. Nobody needs to tell a retailer in Japan or South Korea not to sell imported American merchandise.

China is a state-sponsored economy whose government does not permit private business activity, and especially not by foreign companies, that threaten the interests of the state. China's government tolerates companies like Apple and Boeing selling iPhones and airplanes in China, so long as most of the value is added in China and exports are made to the United States to earn $US for China. If they stop serving China's interests, their assets in China may be confiscated. I worked for an American company whose business was set back for years, and perhaps forever, when it moved its manufacturing operations to China. Its Chinese partner stole them, costing the company $150 million in lost equipment and inventory. The Chinese copied the products the company

37

used to sell in the U.S., so the losses have compounded every year. China's government didn't instigate the confiscation, but neither would it protect the American owner from the Chinese business partner who executed the seizure. China's government perennially promises to open its markets to imports of American products but rarely, if ever, keeps its word.

Most of our free trade treaties with countries like Australia, Canada, Colombia, Morocco, and Peru are mutually beneficial, as is GATT trade with many other countries. Our trade with Canada prospers both countries because we have approximately equal wages, taxes; similar laws; and a common language and culture (in most of Canada) with each country specializing in different areas of complementary trade. Trade with Mexico would be mutually beneficial if Mexicans didn't have much lower incomes than Americans, making it impossible for them to buy most made-in-USA products. Mexico as a labor substitution market was not a good candidate for common market free trade with the United States. We import about 3 million cars from Mexico, transferring 560,000 American auto-worker jobs to that country, while exporting no significant number of U.S. made cars to Mexico --- the reverse of NAFTA-WITH-MEXICO's promise of a balance of trade surplus with Mexico.

The trade deficit in manufactured product has caused the value of manufacturing in the United States to peak in 2007 at 106 and decline in the 17 following years to the current (February 2025) 99.9, as shown in the "How's Manufacturing" reports that can be obtained from the St. Louis Federal Reserve (FRED):

https://fred.stlouisfed.org/series/IPMAN

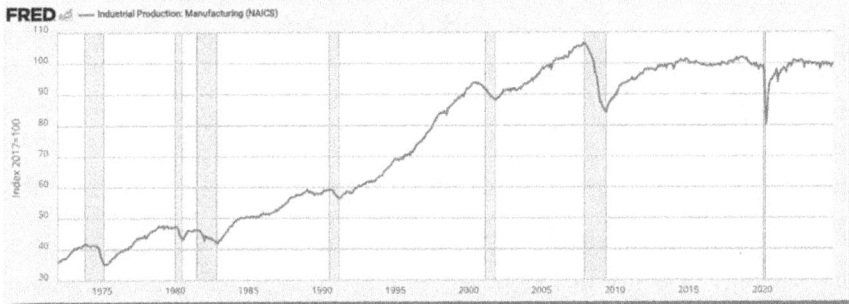

FRED — Industrial Production: Manufacturing (NAICS)

Our economy has shifted away from producing the tangible products we consume and toward financial and recreational services, government employment, and government-funded employment in academia and healthcare, backstopped by $trillions of federal government debt used to cover the trade deficits and fund government employment and social welfare subsidies for people who lost their manufacturing jobs to imports. Our analysis of free trade vs. tariffs must consider whether this shift from manufacturing to services and government-funded employment, combined with a reduction in labor force participation, is offset by buying other countries' manufactured products.

The philosophical debate is over whether other countries have a true competitive advantage over the United States in producing products of superior value at lower costs, or whether trade between countries of vastly disparate in wealth, like the United States importing from China and Mexico, are labor-substitution agreements purposed to enhance multinational corporation profits by producing at a depressed wage scale in poor countries and selling at an inflated price list in developed countries. These treaties become controversial when they disemploy the wealthier countries' workers, fomenting economic distress and political instability.

The Great Recession

The Great Recession of 2008-2015 prompted a re-evaluation of our free trade in the same way   the Great Depression of 1929-1941 prompted a re-evaluation of the Smoot-Hawley tariffs. In neither case was trade or tariffs on trade a primary instigating factor of the calamity. The economy crashed in 1929 and 2008 because it was top-heavy with debt borrowed to fund stock market and real estate speculations at the top of the business cycle when investors should have been selling overvalued assets to pay debts instead of borrowing more, including reckless speculations by banks playing the stock market with their depositors' money. It is difficult to say how much international trade --- tariffs in 1929 and free trade in 2008 --- augmented the collapses, because the primary factors of financial malfeasance at the top of multi-generational business cycles were overpowering.

Nevertheless, the Smoot Hawley tariffs, levied after the Great Depression was underway, created an "every country for itself" idea that may have contributed to the accession of Adolf Hitler to power in Germany and of the Japanese militarists. Hitler started his war to conquer Poland and the Soviet Union, while Japan started its half of the war to conquer China and Southeast Asia. They were wars for economic exploitation of other peoples by stealing their natural resources and forcing them to work as slaves who traded their labor extracting natural resources for Nazi Germany and Imperial Japan in return for being a closed market to purchase the manufactured goods of Germany and Japan at monopoly prices. Thus, it can be credibly argued that the Smoot Hawley tariff added its dose of economic poison to the world even if it did not directly cause the Great Depression.

Likewise, I believe excessive imports from non-reciprocating countries did not cause, but nevertheless intensified, the Great Recession that began in 2008 and did not completely let up until 2016. As the owner of a trade management business, I saw trouble brewing In 1997 when the global economy began to unravel with the Asian financial crisis that devalued currencies of Asian countries. In 1998 it spread to Latin America. The devaluation occurred because workers in these countries do not earn enough to consume the products their labor produces, so their economies must be propped up by exports to the United States. These countries need to rely more on their domestic markets to keep their economies functioning, and when internals go soft, even access to the markets of the United States cannot sustain them.

In summer 1998, I noticed export orders from the United States being cancelled because people and businesses in those countries could no longer afford to purchase American-made products with devalued currencies. The cheap labor advantage of Asian and South American countries was increased by devaluation of their currencies. My clients in the machine manufacturing and chemicals industries began closing their U.S. operations and moving the work overseas, laying off millions of Americans, because those markets were no longer strong enough to buy American exports, and because devaluation of their currencies reduced their workers' wages even further below Americans'. Instead of building product in the United States to export to countries in Lartin America and Asia, American companies moved production to Latin America and Asia (mostly Chin) and imported their products into the United States.

After the currency devaluations, American corporations began dismissing their American employees as a first resort instead of last resort. Instead of working through adverse business conditions as before, they began using adverse business conditions as a pretext for shipping American jobs out of the country. I consulted with a chemical company in 2005 when prices for oil and natural gas tripled, thereby raising their input costs. In prior days, the company would have worked through the price spikes. In 2005 they closed factories, laid off 2,000 American workers, and started buying chemicals from China. Three years later, the Great Recession reduced energy prices to their lowest level in a decade, but by then the factory was shuttered. Henceforth chemicals in the nylon family were purchased from China. American chemical engineers, accountants, computer techs, production planners, and factory hands never went back to work. Companies dumping millions of Americans overboard, to remove the work overseas, did their share of igniting the economic catastrophe:

1. Beginning in the 1990s, millions of American jobs were lost by removal of production to Mexico and China, with importation of product back into the United States. Others were lost to mergers and acquisitions. Some were lost by automation, some to high energy prices, some because of uncertainty after the 9/11 terror attacks, and many by the perennial desire of corporations for cost cutting via layoffs and involuntary early retirements.

2. Companies claimed global trade forced them to let their people go. "We had to reduce our workforce to compete in a global economy." The layoffs happened because corporations wanted to inflate their profit margins and free up cash flow to buy back stock and increase dividends, knowing they could replace American workers with people from cheap-labor countries.

3. Companies that formerly would have worked their way through temporary business problems, like the brief recession that followed the 9/11 attack, and the spike in oil and natural gas prices in 2005-2007, closed their U.S.

factories and moved them to Mexico and China because a 90% discount on labor more than offset high costs of raw materials.

4.   The Republicans and Democrats pressured the Federal Reserve to lower interest rates to zero, hoping to prop up the economy with consumption funded by debt.

5.   Instead of investing in business expansion, too many people and companies purchased overpriced homes and stocks on credit. They did not invest in American businesses to expand employment because American businesses were closing their U.S. operations and moving the work to China and Mexico.

6.   The accumulation of job losses from all causes, including offshoring the industrial economy, caused many homeowners to default on their mortgages. Banks became insolvent and the stock market crashed. The federal government (taxpayers) bailed out the failed banks and some other companies by adding $10 trillion to the national debt.

7.   Even after the bailouts, the jobs-creating side of the economy remained sluggish due to continued offshoring of American jobs to Mexico and China.

Enough voters believed detrimental trade was a substantive cause of the economic collapse to propel Donald Trump, who'd never campaigned for public office, ahead of all the better-known Republican candidate like Jeb Bush, Marco Rubio, John Kasich, and Ted Cruise, to win the Republican nomination in 2016, then defeat Hillary Clinton in the general election. In August 2016, Democrat activist Michael Moore explained why Trump was destined to prevail:

5 Reasons Why Trump Will Win

Michael Moore

Trump is going to focus much of his attention on the four blue states in the Rustbelt of the upper Great Lakes – Michigan, Ohio, Pennsylvania and Wisconsin. Four traditionally Democratic states.... How can the race be this close?

Well maybe it's because he's said (correctly) that the Clintons' support of NAFTA helped to destroy the industrial states of the Upper Midwest. Trump is going to hammer Clinton on this and her support of TPP and other trade policies that have royally [ ]d the people of these four states.

And this is where the math comes in. In 2012, Mitt Romney lost by 64 electoral votes. Add up the electoral votes cast by Michigan, Ohio, Pennsylvania and Wisconsin. It's 64. All Trump needs to win.

A blogger on the ***Daily Kos*** election night log reported:

People are suffering financially in ways that we haven't seen since the 1920s. We are close to losing in this election because democrats who have enough money to be comfy don't see it. Don't know it and refuse to believe it. The country is still poor. The job market is still s----. Bernie tapped into that anger and so did Trump. This was a referendum on poverty and what causes it.

The election of 2024 was decided the same way as in 2016, with Trump winning "The Blue Wall States" whose people were fed up with their jobs going overseas. A Pennsylvania steel worker thanked Trump:

"The president has saved the steel industry. You saved it with tariffs. You're my hero and the greatest president ever. We want to endorse you and give you a hard hat."

Even the staunchest friends of international trade admitted a new era had arrived:

UK prime minister to admit 'globalization is over' in response to Trump tariffs:

U.K. Prime Minister Keir Starmer will announce Sunday [April 6, 2025] that he understands the rationale behind President Donald Trump's tariffs and that the West is entering a new economic era.

"The world has changed, globalization is over and we are now in a new era," the prime minister's office said in a statement to the Sunday Times. "We've got to demonstrate that our approach, a more active Labour government, a more reformist government, can provide the answers for people in every part of this country."

"Trump has done something that we don't agree with, but there's a reason why people are behind him on this," the prime minister's office said in the statement.

Apple's "Taming of the Screw"

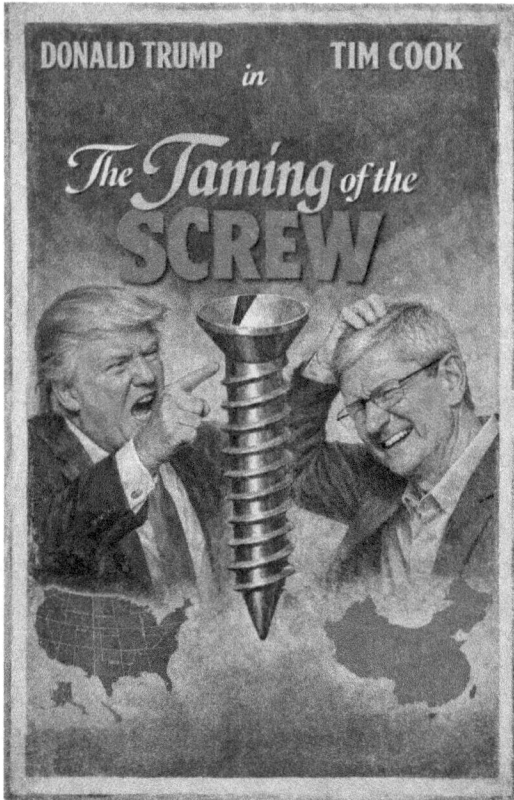

Corporation managements and politicians unfavorably disposed toward working-class Americans have developed a line of propaganda that seeks to justify the offshoring Americans' jobs. The basis of the propaganda is the allegation that Americans, who made the United States the world's preeminent economic power and provided the military muscle that won most of our wars, have become too dumb, lazy, incompetent, and behind the times to manufacture product for a global economy.

Contrived stories are invented to "prove" that American companies had no choice but to move their production to Mexico and

China because Americans no longer knew how to produce technologically advanced products. One of the most infamous is the tale of Apple's tiny screw:

https://macdailynews.com/2019/01/28/a-tiny-screw-shows-why-iphones-wont-be-assembled-in-u-s-a/

A tiny screw shows why iPhones won't be 'Assembled in U.S.A.'

"In 2012, Apple's chief executive, Timothy D. Cook announced that Apple would make a Mac computer in the United States. By the time the computer was ready for mass production, Apple had ordered screws from China."

"But when Apple began making the $3,000 computer in Austin, Tex., it struggled to find enough screws, according to three people who worked on the project and spoke on the condition of anonymity because of confidentiality agreements," Nicas writes. "In China, Apple relied on factories that can produce vast quantities of custom screws on short notice. In Texas, where they say everything is bigger, it turned out the screw suppliers were not."

"Tests of new versions of the computer were hamstrung because a 20-employee machine shop that Apple's manufacturing contractor was relying on could produce at most 1,000 screws a day," Nicas writes. "The screw shortage was one of several problems that postponed sales of the computer for months, the people who worked on the project said. By the time the computer was ready for mass production, Apple had ordered screws from China."

"China is not just cheap. It's a place where, because it's an authoritarian government, you can marshal 100,000 people to work all night for you," said Susan Helper, an economics professor at Case Western

Reserve University in Cleveland and the former chief economist at the Commerce Department.

Ms. Helper said Apple could make more products in the United States if it invested significant time and money and relied more on robotics and specialized engineers instead of large numbers of low-wage line workers. She said government and industry would also need to improve job training and promote the development of a supply-chain infrastructure."

A discerning reader might note that the "tiny screw" story is dubious, and probably a fiction, because Apple went, or pretended to go, to one 20-employee machine shop in one Texas town to ask for screws, instead of putting out a nationwide request for proposal from all the thousands of companies that make billions of screws in the United States. They did not want the public to know they were going to China for cheap labor and because China's government told them they could not sell in China unless they produced there. American companies soon discovered that China's authoritarian government can "marshal 100,000 people to work all night for you," by threatening dire consequences for any who refuse to work long hours for short pay. American companies began moving American jobs to China because it's cheaper to coerce human beings to act like robots than to buy robots that act like people.

As soon as Trump was re-elected on a tariff platform in 2024, Apple instantly found $500 billion in its cashbox to manufacture in the United States:

Apple.com/newsroom/2025/02/apple-will-spend-more-than-500-billion-usd-in-the-us-over-the-next-four-years/

February 24, 2025

Apple will spend more than $500 billion in the U.S. over the next four years

Teams and facilities to expand in Michigan, Texas, California, Arizona, Nevada, Iowa, Oregon, North Carolina, and Washington Plans include a new factory in Texas, doubling the U.S. Advanced Manufacturing Fund, a manufacturing academy, and accelerated investments in AI and silicon engineering

"We are bullish on the future of American innovation, and we're proud to build on our long-standing U.S. investments with this $500 billion commitment to our country's future," said Tim Cook, Apple's CEO.

"From doubling our Advanced Manufacturing Fund, to building advanced technology in Texas, we're thrilled to expand our support for American manufacturing. And we'll keep working with people and companies across this country to help write an extraordinary new chapter in the history of American innovation."

It took the election of Trump and $500 billion for Apple to tame the screw, but now it treads docilely into the manufacturing plants of the USA.

Trade with Mexico

In 1993, Vice President Albert Gore debated business magnate Ross Perot on the ratification of NAFTA-WITH-MEXICO in a nationally televised debate on CNN. Mr. Gore promised creation of jobs for American workers because of an export-driven trade surplus of made-in-USA product he predicted would follow ratification. He promised more American jobs 39 times:

http://ggallarotti.web.wesleyan.edu/govt155/goreperot.htm

*Vice Pres. GORE: **NAFTA will...greatly accelerate [our trade with Mexico]; we will have a larger trade surplus with Mexico than with any country in the entire world***

We'll create more jobs with NAFTA.

He told a story about his friend who makes tires:

...This can be illustrated by the story of a good friend of mine that I grew up with, named Gordon Thompson ...He makes tires for a

living...his job will be more secure, they'll make more tires, they'll be able to sell more tires. Mexico bought 750,000 new cars last year. The Big Three sold them only 1,000, because they have the same barriers against our cars. Those barriers will be eliminated by NAFTA. We'll sell 60,000, not 1,000, in the first year after NAFTA. Every one of those cars has four new tires and one spare.

I believe Mr. Gore was sincere in making those forecasts. I also believed NAFTA-WITH-MEXICO would deliver on its promise of trade surpluses and jobs. I wrote my Congresspersons and Senators and asked them to ratify it. I thought of Mexicans as good neighbors who work hard with humble pride, making them a worthy addition to our North American family of the USA and Canada. Others thought so too. My father talked about his labor union friend who asked President Clinton not to sign NAFTA-WITH-MEXICO. According to my Dad's friend, President Clinton said, "I know this may cause union families to think less well of me, but it's the right thing to do." It was one of the few things Republicans and Democrats agreed on.

Our motives in signing NAFTA-WITH-MEXICO were well meaning in believing it would benefit our workers by creating more jobs at higher wages through trade surpluses with Mexico. When Mr. Gore made those promises of trade surpluses and jobs for Americans, we had a modest $1.6 billion trade surplus with Mexico. Alas, as soon as the treaty was ratified, the trade went instantly into deficit, increasing every year until it reached $170 billion in 2024 and $200 billion in 2025. It is our third largest trade deficit, after China and the European Union. Few cars or tires made in the USA were ever exported to Mexico, while we are now importing nearly three million cars *from* Mexico, putting 560,000 American auto workers out of work and impoverishing those who kept their jobs at automobile component suppliers, as *The Wall Street Journal* reported in 2015:

At an American Axle & Manufacturing Holdings Inc. car-parts factory in Three Rivers, some new hires are paid as little as about $10 an hour, roughly equivalent to what the local Wal-Mart will pay. John Childers, a 38-year-old assembly-line stocker, said he is grateful for the job but finds it tough to get by on the money he and his fiancée make at the plant.

"Lower class is what we are," he says. "Let's be honest."

Mexico was by far the biggest supplier of car parts to the U.S. last year, accounting for 34% of the imports, followed by China with 13%. Imports from China have more than doubled since 2008. Those from Mexico are up 86%.

Nor did Mr. Gore's tire-making friend prosper by exporting tires to Mexico. Odds are he lost his job when the U.S. tire industry relocated *to* Mexico:

https://www.wsj.com/articles/goodyear-to-invest-550-million-in-new-plant-in-central-mexico-1429812017

Goodyear to Invest $550 Million in New Plant in Central Mexico

Goodyear joins an avalanche of component makers pouring into Mexico to supply those assembly plants. Employment in the auto-supplier sector in Mexico is expected to grow from 700,000 to one million in the next few years, according to INA, the industry's national association.

The trade statistics current through 2023 tell the story of NAFTA-WITH-MEXICO's inversion from an anticipated common market with the United States and Canada, to a labor substitution market for auto companies in the USA and Canada:

https://www.trade.gov/country-commercial-guides/mexico-automotive-industry

Table 1: Mexico Passenger Vehicle Sales in Mexico
(Figures in Thousands of Vehicles)

	2019	2020	2021	2022	2023 (Est.)
Total Local Production	3,811	3,040	2,979	3,308	3,526
Total Exports	3,388	2,681	2,706	2,865	3,071
Total Imports	906.7	764.5	991.3	1,176	1,360
Imports from the U.S.	126.0	75.8	84.5	99.1	113.7
Imports Used Vehicles	159.4	124.2	167.0	199.2	231.4
Total Market Size*	1,329	1,123.5	1,264.3	1,619	1,815
Exchange Rates	19.26	20.00	20.28	20.12	18.40
Exchange Rates	19.26	20.00	20.28	20.12	18.40

*Total market size = (total local production + imports) - exports
Source: Mexican Automotive Industry Association (AMIA) and ITA Office of Transportation and Machinery

In 2023, Mexico produced 3,526,000 motor vehicles, exporting 3,071,000 to the United States United States, while importing 113,000 made-in-USA vehicles --- a ratio of 27-to-1. Mexico imported 1,360,000 from other countries, mostly from Japan, China, and South Korea. Thus, Mexican auto workers sell 87% of the cars they produced to other countries, mostly to the United States, whle buying only 8% of their cars from the United States. Mexico is a labor substitution market to disemploy Amerian workers, not a common market for products made by American workers.

As a result of NAFTA, Mexico, not the United States, became the North American powerhouse of motor vehicle exports, because 3 million of the 3.5 million cars made in Mexico are sold in the United States:

https://www.americaeconomia.com/en/node/288010

Mexico is positioned as the third largest automotive exporter worldwide

Thursday, August 1, 2024 - 12:00

Fuente: Reuters

Last year, Mexican exports grew 22.5% to US$158 billion, surpassing those of Japan and the United States, which rose 16.3% and 13%, respectively.

Mexico rose from fourth to third position among the largest automotive exporters from 2022 to 2023, according to data from the World Trade Organization (WTO).

Comparing 2023 with 2013, Chinese automotive exports grew 270%, an unprecedented speed, while the other main exporters showed the following advances: Mexico (90.4%), the European Union (25.7%), the United States (15.6%) and Japan (3.3%).

In 2024, GM assembled over 889,000 vehicles in Mexico, exporting 830,630 units—653,200 shipped to the United States, a 23% increase compared to 2023 Notable production figures included 234,681 units of the Chevrolet Equinox SUV, as well as significant volumes of the Silverado and Sierra pickup trucks. GM also led Mexico's electric vehicle production with 99,529 units, accounting for nearly 60% of the country's total EV output.

GM exports 95% of what it produces in Mexico to other countries, and 79% of what it exports is to the USA. Mexico is not a consumer market for U.S. cars. It's a labor substitution market to dis-employ U.S. workers.

In Mexico, GM operates manufacturing plants in Ramos Arizpe (Coahuila), Silao (Guanajuato), and San Luis Potosí (SLP), employing *over 25,000 people. In 2023, GM produced 722,631 units and made purchases from over 600 suppliers in Mexico totaling $28 billion.*

Nissan followed GM with 669,941 units produced at its manufacturing plants, an 8.8% increase compared to the 615,751 vehicles manufactured in 2023.This year, the Japanese company expanded its portfolio by starting production of the new Nissan Kicks 2025 and celebrated the milestone of assembling 16 million vehicles in Mexico.

Stellantis ranked third with 419,426 units manufactured at its facilities in Saltillo, Coahuila, and Toluca, State of Mexico.

Ford increased its production in Mexico by 5.9% in 2024, manufacturing 386,776 units compared to 365,365 in 2023. The U.S. automaker announced a $273 million investment in its Irapuato, Guanajuato plant to produce Primary Motor Units for its Mustang Mach-E, which is manufactured at its Cuautitlán Izcalli plant.

Volkswagen produced 382,312 vehicles manufactured at its Puebla plant, representing a 9.5% year-over-year increase compared to 349,227 units in 2023.

...significant production plans in Mexico include KIA and Toyota. In 2024, KIA invested $408 million in Nuevo León to expand its operational capacity. Toyota announced a $1.45 billion investment to strengthen operations at its plants in Baja California and Guanajuato for producing the next-generation Tacoma and Tacoma Hybrid Electric Vehicle (HEV).

So much for NAFTA being a bonanza for U.S. exports. It's even worse than it looks because much of what we supposedly "export" to Mexico are parts assembled in Mexico then reshipped to the United States. Only the manufacturer benefits by using the border as a gateway to cheap labor, inflating profit margins by beating Americans out of their jobs.

Mr. Gore also promised that NAFTA would make Mexico a Jeffersonian Democracy of free politics as well as free markets:

We ought to thank our lucky stars that the Mexican people have had the vision and courage to strike out on the American path toward the ideas of Thomas Jefferson, toward democracy, toward free markets, and now they just want to know 'Can we take 'yes' for an answer?'

Since then, Mexicans have voted in socialist presidents and congresses, although democracy has been maintained, and no significant harm has come to American businesses operating in Mexico. It is possible that NAFTA, and now USMCA, has pumped enough money into Mexico, with millions of Mexicans earning $4 / hour making product sold in the United States, to save the country from complete subjugation by drug cartels. Nevertheless, Mexico has devalued its currency 70% relative to the dollar since NAFTA was enacted. Their government had to devalue the wages of their people in $US equivalents to remain attractive as an export hub. The devaluation of the currency makes it even more difficult for Mexicans to afford buying made-in-USA product nullifying the promise of Mexico becoming a market for U.S. exports.

In his first term, Trump attempted to reform NAFTA-WITH-MEXICO by changing its rules and renaming it USMCA. USCMA, ratified by the three nations in October 2020, raised the North American content requirement from 62.5% to 75% to qualify products for tariff-free trade between the three countries. The 75% North American content requirement is purposed to inhibit European and Asian product from infiltrating into NAFTA countries duty free via Mexico. It focuses the treaty on being what it should be: a **North American** trading block. It requires North American steel to be used in auto manufacturing. It mandates a minimum wage of $16 / hour on 40% of Mexico's auto production, to limit the amount of work that can be done at Mexico's average rate of $4 /hour.

Trump's renegotiated USMCA contrasts with the now-defunct Trans-Pacific Partnership (TPP) that would have subverted NAFTA by *lowering* duty-free content requirement from 62.5% to 45%, thereby allowing Chinese-sourced product of up to 55% content to enter the USA, Canada, and Mexico duty free. USMCA's revised terms persuaded foreign car makers to move manufacturing to North America:

https://www.wsj.com/articles/auto-makers-consider-shifting-more-manufacturing-to-north-america-1538737201?mod=hp_lead_pos2

Within days of the U.S. and Canada reaching a pact to replace the roughly 25-year-old North American Free Trade Agreement, executives at several foreign car makers said they are considering changes to their supply chains that would shift more auto-parts manufacturing work to the U.S., Canada and Mexico.

"We will allocate more U.S. production for the U.S. market," BMW AG CEO Harald Krüger told reporters at the Paris Motor Show this week. He said that the German car maker already sources many parts in the region, but the new trade pact will accelerate a shift in investment.

Chinese companies moved their operations to Mexico to access the U.S. market with products built with Mexican labor, thereby meeting the USMCA's 75% North American content requirement:

https://www.bbc.com/news/business-68825118

How Chinese firms are using Mexico as a backdoor to the US.

21 April 2024

Will Grant: BBC Mexico correspondent, Monterrey

Manufacturing in Mexico allows Chinese firm Man Wah to get past US tariffs.

The reclining armchairs and plush leather sofas coming off the production line at Man Wah Furniture's factory in Monterrey are 100% "Made in Mexico".

They're destined for large retailers in the US, like Costco and Walmart. But the company is from China, its Mexican manufacturing plant built with Chinese capital.

The triangular relationship between the US, China and Mexico is behind the buzzword in Mexican business: nearshoring.

Man Wah is one of scores of Chinese companies to relocate to industrial parks in northern Mexico in recent years, to bring production closer to the US market. As well as saving on shipping, their final product is considered completely Mexican - meaning Chinese firms can avoid the US tariffs and sanctions imposed on Chinese goods amid the continuing trade war between the two countries.

As the company's general manager, Yu Ken Wei, shows me around its vast site, he says the move to Mexico has made economic and logistical sense.

Chinese companies still extract profits from the differential between labor costs in Mexico and selling prices in the United States. However, it is better that our neighbors in Mexico should increase their wealth from American trade deficits than Chinese workers. It would be better still if the companies were owned by Americans and Mexicans instead of Chinese, but at least the work is done in Mexico, the Chinese subsidiary is taxed in Mexico, and contracts for plant supplies and maintenance made with Mexican vendors.

However, the wage differential between $40 / hour in the USA and $4 / hour in Mexico will continue to siphon jobs out of the United States, the "giant sucking sound" Ross Perot forecast in 1993. To slow that down, Trump imposed the 25% tariffs on motor vehicles imported from Mexico and 50% on steel and aluminum, the only tariffed exceptions in USMCA. Whether other sectors of the Mexican economy should be tariffed to slow the ballooning trade deficit is a question, because free trade with Mexico was sold to the public and Congress on the false promise that ***NAFTA will...greatly accelerate [our trade with Mexico]; we will have a larger trade surplus with Mexico than with any country in the entire world*** and Trump was twice elected on the promise to prevent every industrial job from going south of the border.

Trade with China

Mexico is as good a neighbor as its difficult circumstances allow and would be inclined to trade fairly with us if its people were paid the same as Americans and had money to purchase made-in-USA products, like our beneficial trade with Canada. China's government only permits its people to buy American-branded products made in China, with Chinese business partners having access to the technical specifications of the products, to copy them as Chinese-branded products if they want to.

As mentioned, I worked for an American industrial company that outsourced its manufacturing to China. Its Chinese business partner confiscated the plant, the production machinery, and started making knock-off products and flooding the U.S. market with them The company lost $150 million in confiscated plant and equipment and recurring losses of sales taken by knock-off products. We should expect confiscation of the assets of every U.S. company in China if we should have a falling out with Taiwan, or another COVID disease negligent Chinese operatives create in a lab and release into the world. In the meantime, China's government is perpetrating millions of cyberattacks against our businesses and government agencies daily to steal information on political and economic processes.

As with Mexico, free trade advocates are backpaddling their theory that China will ever become an export market for American manufactured products. They are now touting China as a market for our exports of "beef and soybeans." But in truth China rarely buys much of anything from the USA, not even beef, touted as our great export of the future. Back in 2003 China's government fooled President George W. Bush into letting them into the World Trade Organization in return for promising to "buy millions of tons of U.S. beef." They never bought so much as a single ounce for fourteen years:

http://www.feedstuffs.com/markets/us-beef-exports-china-increasing-after-14-year-absence

In June 2017, the U.S. began shipping beef to China after a 14-year ban that was enacted after the discovery of isolated cases of bovine spongiform...

The Chinese government claimed they found a "mad cow" protein in one steak and banned the importation of all U.S. beef for fourteen years! How much product would the Chinese sell in the USA, if we banned the importation of Chinese-made goods every time a defect is found in one of their products? They would sell none if we penalized them for deficiency in quality standards, given that most products we import from China are of abysmal quality, like construction materials filled with cardboard, poorly alloyed screws that rust and torque out, small engines that seize up as soon as they're turned on, and lawn mower blades that won't hold an edge.

In 2023 the Chinese bought $29 billon of agricultural exports from the United States, about 10% as much as our year's trade deficit of $279 billion:

https://www.fas.usda.gov/data/trade

To preempt Trump from raising tariffs, the Chinese government permitted the companies it controls to buy $1.61 billion of American beef, less than what South Korea, with 1/28th China's population buys. Over half what China buys from us is soybeans, a crop our government subsidizes with price supports. The rest of our farm exports to China have been stagnant or declining in recent years, falling to $17 billion in 2025 and expected to decline to $9 billion in 2026. Our Chamber of

Commerce complains incessantly about tariffs reducing our farm exports to China --- that are really being reduced because countries like Brazil grow soybeans cheaper than we do --- while ignoring the 70,000 factories and nearly six million well-paying jobs in the high-value industries that have been removed to China, including much of the chemical industry I consulted for.

In recent years a new myth has developed that China and the rest of Asia are an untapped market for American "services." Our bankers thought they could peddle the same financial scams in China that wrecked our economy in 2008, that had to be bailed out with $10 trillion of public debt. Of course, China's government never allowed American bankers offer "financial services" their banks can emulate. Nor do Chinese companies pay much in the way of "services" royalties when they pirate our software. At times, 90% of Microsoft Windows copies running in China are pirated. Microsoft is giving away Windows in China because the Chinese won't pay for them. The largest "services" we sell to China are tuition charged by our universities so that owners of Chinse companies can send their children to American universities that Americans cannot afford, unless they take a lifetime of student debt.

For China, trade with the U.S. is purposed to extract wealth from our country to increase China's trade dominance with the world. Chinese companies used our trade deficit dollars to lease the ports on the Panama Canal and build a bridge over the canal that can be used to block it if we have a falling out with China:

Panama Renews 25-year concession to Hutchison's Panama Ports [A Chinese-owned company]

Panama Maritime Authority (AMP) authorized the automatic renewal of a 25-year concession to Panama Ports Company (PPC) on June 23, [2021] despite some resistance.

China is building a bridge over the canal:

China to Proceed with Fourth Bridge over Panama Canal June 15, 2024

Panama, together with the Chinese consortium made up of state-owned China Communications Construction Company (CCCC) and China Harbour Engineering Company (CHEC), signed an addendum to resume construction "in the coming months" of the fourth bridge over the Panamanian interoceanic canal, La Estrella de Panamá reported.

72% of the traffic through that canal is to and from American ports. China should have no business controlling the transit through it or building the infrastructure in and around it. Other ports in Latin America and the Caribbean are leased by Chinese companies via the "Belt and Road" projects linking Latin American and African resources funded with our trade deficit dollars.

https://dialogo-americas.com/articles/chinas-network-of-ports-grows-in-latin-america/

China's Network of Ports Grows in Latin America

According to a late 2022 study by the U.S.-based national security and defense think tank Center for a Secure Free Society (SFS), the number of Chinese-owned or operated ports worldwide has increased considerably.

China's foothold in some 40 ports in Latin America from Peru to Mexico, combined with 11 satellite ground stations in Argentina, Brazil,

Bolivia, and Venezuela, allows the country to have strategic locations in the Western Hemisphere, the SFS report indicates.

"China does not make random investments or choose geopolitical positions that aren't aligned with its strategic objectives," Daniel Pou, director of the Citizen Security Data Analysis Center of the Dominican Republic, told Diálogo on January 4.

Many of the Chinese state-owned companies involved in these infrastructure investment and development projects have ties to the Chinese People's Liberation Army (PLA), the SFS report says. China's military force, in support of Chinese companies' economic expansion, has been cautiously moving forward for a long time, Uruguay's content platform L21 reported.

During his second term, Trump requested Panama's government to eject the Chinese from control of the Panama Canal:

Panama's top court annulled key port contracts held by Hong Kong's CK Hutchison to operate at either side of the Panama Canal.

China on Friday said it would be taking "necessary measures" following a ruling by Panama's Supreme Court, that Chinese control of Panama Canal ports was unconstitutional.

In the United States, Chinese are buying houses and apartments around universities to rent to American students, burdening them with student loan debt, some paying Chinese landlords. They own 380,000 acres of American farmland, some near military bases. They have used our trade deficit dollars to fund the creation of an unlicensed virology lab in California, like the one in Wuhan, China, that probably spawned the COVID-19 plague:

/story/news/nation/2023/07/31/illegal-lab-california-infectious-mice/70502532007/

'Fairly shocking': Secret medical lab in California stored bioengineered mice laden with COVID

Thao Nguyen, Saleen Martin

USA TODAY

Inside the warehouse in Reedley, California, furniture, medical devices and other materials were improperly stored.

A monthslong investigation into a rural California warehouse uncovered an illegal laboratory filled with infectious agents, medical waste and hundreds of mice bioengineered "to catch and carry the COVID-19 virus," according to Fresno County authorities.

Health and licensing said Monday that Prestige Biotech, a Chinese medical company registered in Nevada, was operating the unlicensed facility in Reedley, California, a small city about 24 miles southeast of Fresno. According to Reedley City Manager Nicole Zieba, had a goal of being a diagnostics lab.

"They never had a business license," Zieba told USA TODAY. "The city was completely unaware that they were in this building, operating under the cover of night."

Three years later, they are still sneaking biolabs in here:

https://www.nysun.com/article/possible-las-vegas-bio-lab-is-linked-to-a-chinese-man-jailed-in-california

February 5, 2026

A suspected bio lab uncovered in a Las Vegas Airbnb rental is now linked to a similar 2023 incident in Reedley, California, police say.

A housekeeper first alerted the Las Vegas Metropolitan Police Department about the possible lab last month. The woman, identified in court papers as Kelly, told authorities that she was hired by a property manager to clean various short-term rentals, including the home that contained the possible bio lab.

And allegedly trying to smuggle in plague viruses to kill our agriculture:

https://www.dailymail.co.uk/news/article-15269547/University-Michigan-foreign-bioweapons-spying.html

Inside China's bioweapons plot that transformed Michigan's 'Big House' into ground zero of covert warfare

Published: 07:44 EST, 2 December 2025 | Updated: 11:11 EST, 2 December 2025

The University of Michigan is supposed to be the pride of the Midwest.

A 200-year-old college that has been dubbed a 'Public Ivy,' the school is steeped in tradition, pride and academic excellence. It is also the home of the Wolverines and the Big House, the largest stadium in America.

Now, the beloved school is increasingly seen as a back door for Beijing - a soft target for Chinese operatives, covert networks and alleged plots involving genetically modified parasites and crop-killing fungi.

The potential for Chinese bioweapons attacks on the United States continue:

On November 5, 2025 federal agents charged three Chinese nationals - Xu Bai, 28, Fengfan Zhang, 27, and Zhiyong Zhang, 30 - with conspiring to smuggle biological materials into the US while working at a University of Michigan (U-M) research lab.

They were the newest names in a disturbing string of cases involving Chinese nationals allegedly moving dangerous biological samples through campus labs under the guise of academic research.

According to the DOJ, Bai and Fengfan Zhang allegedly received multiple shipments from China between 2024 and this year containing 'concealed biological materials related to round worms.' The parasites are known to infect both humans and livestock.

The samples allegedly had 'genetic modifications,' according to notes in the suspect packages, and were shipped to them while they worked at U-M's Shawn Xu laboratory, prosecutors say.

This is on top of China's routine spying and sabotage in the U.S.

https://www.foxnews.com/us/secret-service-dismantles-telecommunications-threat-near-un-general-assembly-new-york

The U.S. Secret Service said Tuesday that it "dismantled a network of electronic devices located throughout the New York tristate area that were used to conduct multiple telecommunications-related threats directed towards senior U.S. government officials."

The devices were concentrated within 35 miles of the ongoing United Nations General Assembly meeting in New York.

"This network had the potential to disable cellphone towers and essentially shut down the cellular network in New York City," Matt

McCool, the special agent in charge of the Secret Service's New York field office, said in a video released Tuesday.

The Secret Service said it found "more than 300 co-located SIM servers and 100,000 SIM cards across multiple sites."

"In addition to carrying out anonymous telephonic threats, these devices could be used to conduct a wide range of telecommunications attacks. This includes disabling cell phone towers, enabling denial of services attacks and facilitating anonymous, encrypted communication between potential threat actors and criminal enterprises," the Secret Service said. "While forensic examination of these devices is ongoing, early analysis indicates cellular communications between nation-state threat actors and individuals that are known to federal law enforcement."

Do we really want to continue funding China's aggressions against the United States with our trade deficit dollars? Would it be safe to do business with China under any circumstances?

The Trans-Pacific Partnership

The Trans-Pacific Partnership (TPP) was a proposed trading bloc of 12 countries, touted by its U.S. multinational corporations and the politicians they fund as a vehicle to open Asian markets to U.S. exports, while supposedly presenting a united front against China's predatory trade polices. The countries proposed for TPP were the United States, Australia, Brunei, Canada, Chile, Japan, Malaysia, Mexico, New Zealand, Peru, Singapore, and Vietnam. The United States already has free trade with Australia, Canada, Chile, Mexico, Peru, and Singapore. We have GATT trade with the rest, supposedly to minimize tariffs.

So, what was the TPP supposed to accomplish that bilateral free trade agreements plus the default of GATT trade between countries couldn't? The treaty was really purposed to help the other countries infiltrate Chinese products into the United States duty-free, as the Japanese business press explained:

http://thediplomat.com/2015/10/what-the-tpp-means-for-japan/

What the TPP means for Japan

*Second, the [**Japanese**] auto industry will benefit from a phase-in in the reduction of tariffs on their exports. Also, they will be allowed to buy more parts for their products from Asia, including, significantly, from countries not in the TPP.* ***The "rule of origin"***http://ajw.asahi.com/article/behind_news/politics/AJ2015100500 05 ***requires only 45 percent of the vehicle to be made in the TPP zone; in the North America Free Trade Agreement (NAFTA), the equivalent figure is 62.5 percent.***

Being able to buy cheaper parts from countries such as China and then sell vehicles with reduced tariffs to markets such as the U.S. is good for the Japanese auto industry.

The usual questions come to mind:

- How would we benefit by allowing Japan to source 55% of a product's value in China and sell it in the United States tariff-free?
- How would it benefit the United States to replace the 62.5% North American content required for tariff-free trade between us and Canada and Mexico with a new treaty requiring only 45% of the content to be made in those countries?
- If we want to confront China's unfair trade practices, why not do it directly, without involving an international trade bureaucracy that doesn't represent our interests?

The treaty became moribund when these objections were raised during President Trump's first administration. The question remains of why every trade treaty written by politicians funded by multinational corporations is so terrible for the United States. Perhaps it is because these treaties are written only for the benefit of multinational corporations that week tor replace their American employees with Chinese.

Do Trade Deficits matter?

The friends of free trade sold their treaties to the public and to Congress on the promise of trade surpluses for the United States, recalling Vice President Gore's 1993 promise:

"NAFTA will...greatly accelerate [our trade with Mexico]; we will have a larger trade surplus with Mexico than with any country in the entire world."

Gore promised surpluses because he believed they would create jobs for American workers producing product to export to other countries, the traditional reason for wanting foreign trade. When he said that in 1993, our trade with Mexico was modestly in surplus of $1.6 billion dollars. Today Mexico is our third largest trade *deficit* country, with our top seven trade deficit countries costing us $1.06 *trillion* leaving the country in 2024, as shown below in $billions:

Country	Exports	Imports	Deficits
China	143.5	438.9	-295.4
European Union	370.2	605.8	-235.6
Mexico	334.0	505.8	-171.8
Vietnam	13.1	136.6	-123.5
Japan	79.7	148.2	-68.5
South Korea	65.5	131.5	-66.0
India	41.7	87.4	-45.7
Total			**-1,006.5**

When the promised trade surpluses inverted into trade deficits and job losses, the champions of free trade reversed their goal posts by purporting to believe that trade deficits and job losses were beneficial. They claimed the trade deficit is because we're wealthier than other

71

countries, so of course we buy more from them than from us. Then why did Free traders claim we would have trade surpluses with low-wage countries, if they knew it was impossible? Did they only want trade treaties according to how many American workers they could replace with cheap labor foreigners making product to import into the United States and sold at inflated markups?

The friends of free trade then claimed the trade deficit dollars we send to other countries must always return to the United States, to be invested in high technology enterprises superior to manufacturing. They said don't worry about trade deficits destroying current investments when billion-dollar factories are shuttered and workers with billions of hours invested in developing industrial skills are idled and lifetimes of accumulated wealth nullified. According to them, all losses in financial and human capital will be invested in new technologies like AI; the more trade deficit dollars we send abroad, the faster our new industries will develop In accounting lingo, their slogan became, "Our capital account must balance the trade deficit."

But in fact, there is no necessity for the trade deficit dollars to return to the United States, because our dollar may be used to settle personal and business transactions anywhere, often in ways detrimental to our interests. Trade deficit dollars sent to China can be transferred to Russia to buy oil. They can be transferred from Russia to Iran and North Korea to buy weapons to attack Ukraine. They can be transferred from Iran to the terrorist organizations that attack Israel. They can be used by China, North Korea, and Iran to hire nuclear and rocket scientists to build nuclear weapons and mate them to missiles that may one day be used against us. They can be used to bribe the leaders of other countries to favor doing business with China and other trade deficit partners, while excluding American products.

Even when trade deficit dollars return to the United States, they are often used to buy U.S Treasury debt paying interest extracted by taxes on our citizens. They may fund purchases of American companies' stock and interest-bearing bonds, or buy real estate foreigners rent back to Americans, making us landlords in our own country. Is it a beneficial trade when American family breadwinners out of work with imports so foreigners can help our domestic speculators inflate the stock market, then crash it when it becomes overvalued? Foreigners spending trade deficit dollars bid up the price of real estate and either rent properties back to Americans or leave them vacant as idle investments, as *The Wall Street Journal* reports:

https://www.wsj.com/real-estate/la-vacant-homes-china-international-homeowners-ab30fa88?mod=hp_lead_pos8

A Sore Spot in L.A.'s Housing Crisis: Foreign-Owned Homes Sitting Empty

International buyers, particularly from China, have contributed to the hundreds of thousands of vacant properties in Los Angeles County

By Rebecca Picciotto Feb. 9, 2025 9:00 pm ET

Foreigners using our trade deficit dollars to take homes off the market makes it harder for American citizens to buy homes. Our trade deficit dollars are likewise used to make housing unaffordable for people in smaller markets in Canada, New Zealand, and Australia:

https://www.wsj.com/articles/western-cities-want-to-slow-flood-of-chinese-home-buying-nothing-works-1528294587

Western Cities Want to Slow Flood of Chinese Home Buying. Nothing Works.

Governments from Vancouver to Sydney to Toronto are using taxes and other restrictions to tackle real estate bubbles

Sydney's home state of New South Wales doubled its foreign-buyers tax to 8% in July 2017, but that didn't arrest demand.... Chinese property buying is an "unstoppable juggernaut..."

Trade deficit dollars are used to bribe our politicians, government bureaucrats, business leaders, media, and academic people to work secretly for China and against the United States. For example, The Department of Justice reported that Harvard University's Dean of Chemical Biology was a paid Chinese agent who surreptitiously sold the university's biomedical research to China. This is why our elites were so reluctant to admit that Covid was likely to have originated in a Chinese laboratory. The leading politicians of both parties are paid millions by companies affiliated with China's communist party, including a former president and his family. We must assume our trade deficit dollars can and will be used against us by corrupting our business, academic, and political leaders.

Champions of trade deficits claim that foreigners are doing us a favor by using trade deficit dollars to buy our government's debt. But when foreigners buy our government debt it is because they are buying cashflow from the interest we and our descendants must pay in the future. We are levying future taxes on our children and grandchildren, without their consent, to pay back what we have borrowed to fund our present-day consumption of foreign-made products that will soon be in landfill, leaving behind no permanent value. Foreign purchases of American corporations' stocks and bonds likewise transfer the future income streams and capital appreciation of these assets away from our children and to the children of foreigners. Foreign purchases of American real estate inflate property values, making it more difficult for

74

Americans to find affordable housing. Our trade deficit dollars are being used by Chinese to buy out the smaller real estate markets of Canada, Australian, and New Zealand cities and renting them back to the locals at extortionate rates:

Yet another line of trade-deficits-are-good school is that we have trade deficits because "Americans buy too much instead of saving our money. If we didn't consume so much, the trade deficit would be smaller." This is like saying that if your car is stolen it's your fault because you spent too much money buying it instead of putting your money in the bank. Free Traders also take the opposite tack of claiming trade deficits are good because they boost consumption of low-priced imports. However, imports may destroy more consuming power than they augment because people who lose their jobs to trade lose 100% of their income and cannot afford to buy anything.

Then there is the macroeconomic effect on our economy. Aa previously discussed, the trade deficit in manufactured product caused the value of manufacturing in the United States to peak in 2007 and decline in the 18 years that followed.

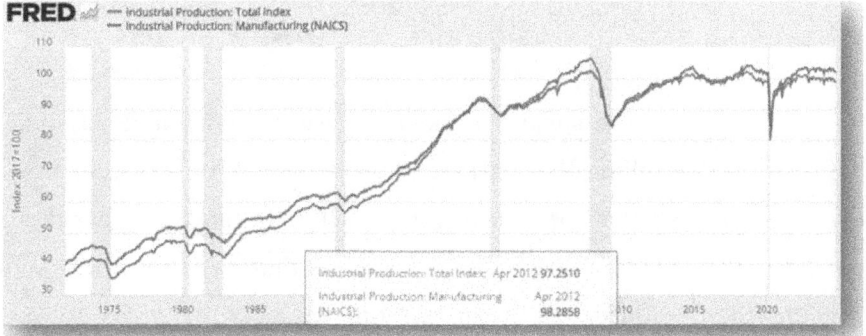

In the 23 years from 1977 to 2000, the United States GDP grew at 3.4% compounded (adjusting for inflation) and in the 23 years from 2000 to 2023 it grew at 2.13%, during a time when we were expanding the population rapidly by immigration. What was it that reduced our growth by more than a third?

Our economic growth per year before admitting China to the World Trade Organization for zero-tariff imports in 2000 was 3.4% per year. After we began shipping our industry to China, economic growth fell to 2.1% per year from 2000 to 2024 ---- while the national debt increased 6% per year, in part due to the decline of tax revenue from shipping so much industry and so many jobs overseas, combined with the necessity to backstop the unemployment caused by trade deficits and job losses.

The friends of free trade have taken to claiming that the trade deficit in manufactured goods is offset by trade surplus in services they claim are the "new economy." We do run a trade surplus of $295 billion that offsets 24% of the material goods trade deficit:

	Goods	Services	Total G + S
2024 Exports	2,083.2	1,107.4	3,190.6
2024 Imports	3,296.2	812.2	4,108.4
Balance	-1,213.0	295.2	-917.8

Even with the surplus in services, we have a combined trade deficit of $917.8 billion that extracts $2,700 of wealth every year from every one of the 340,000,000 people in the United States. Furthermore, our largest "export of services" are foreigners touring the country and sending their children to American universities. It's great to see foreigners spending money on sightseeing in the USA and sending their children to universities here, perhaps to learn American values. These are trade dollars taken away from American wage-earning families who would like to be able to take their children on tours of the United States scenic areas increasingly jammed with foreigners who profited from our trade deficits. They want to be able to afford to send their children to American colleges and universities that have become inflated with costs to enroll foreign students.

The trade deficit is also a knowledge deficit. When industries leave the country, we lose the knowledge of how to make these products. Because the future development of products depends on improvement of what is produced now, we lose the future value of the industry as well as its present when we offshore it. The knowledge of the industry and how to improve it for the future develops in other countries, not the United States. Over time, we fall further behind other countries, and our companies demand $hundreds of billions of subsidies "to catch up with China If we had given away our horse-drawn carriage industry to China in 1900, that is where the motor vehicle industry would have developed, because that would be where the vehicle engineers and skilled workers were.

A national security threat develops when we offshore the products we require for our civil and military necessities, as Alexander Hamilton mentioned in his Report on Manufacturers. How are we going to "deter China" when we have removed so much industry form this country that we nowadays trickle ships, aircraft, missiles, and fighting vehicles in single-digit quantities a month, when we needed them by the hundreds and thousands a month to win World War II? Granted, today's weapons are much more powerful than the ones of World War II, but they are also expended or destroyed very quickly and cannot be replaced with our low-capacity industrial base.

The more we relocate our manufacturing overseas, the more our economy depends on government-funded employment in state, federal, and local bureaucracies, and in government-funded healthcare and "education." In 2023, our combined state, federal, and local government employment grew at the fastest rate since 1968. California is said to have reported that 96% of jobs created in that state in recent years are in state government. If we continue to move our manufacturing overseas, how are we going to generate the tax revenue to fund the increasing share of the government-funded economy? We are now running $2 trillion federal budget deficits, including $800 billion servicing the $37 trillion of accumulated debt, almost as much as we spend on national defense. How is that going to be funded in a hollowed-out economy deficient in payrolls and taxes?

The most detrimental effect of trade deficits is the human cost of people spending the bulk of their lives without work after their jobs are shipped out of the country and handed off to foreign workers building the same products Americans used to make, and the companies importing those foreign-made products back into the United States where the Americans who used to make them can no longer afford them. Free traders do not want to admit that trade destroys jobs. They do not want to talk about the destruction of American families in the de-industrialized cities that look worse than anything in the Third World, inhabited by people living from crime and welfare because the job opportunities were removed in too short a time for them to adjust. The friends of free trade at first tried to blame the job losses on "robots and automation:" but this argument became too ludicrous to proliferate after it became obvious that companies move jobs to cheap labor counties to *avoid* spending money on robots and automation in the United States.

The friends of free trade then pretended to believe there is no loss of employment through trade because people laid off in factories can "learn to code." This is an over-optimistic view of the way life works. People put out of their jobs in late career cannot easily transfer their skills to other lines of work. They are not going to "learn to code," a years-long process of education and experience, especially not when high-tech companies are loading up on foreigners on H1-B visas who crowd out American tech workers. The alternative is work in government bureaucracies or government-funded healthcare and academia, the fastest growing sector or our economy in the free trade era.

Then there is the social cost of unemployment. When Americans are unemployed by imports, they lose their dignity and spirit. Having no means to support their families, they turn to substance abuse and suicide. Their children's future may be constrained by their parents' inability to educate them. Families whose breadwinners are unemployed become laden with social pathologies. Our politics becomes radicalized as 'those left behind" seek redress of their grievances through extremist candidates who advocate the forcible redistribution of wealth by government.

The Globalist trading system was built on the principle of the United States creating public debt to fund purchases of foreign products with trade deficit dollars, while corporations destroyed the jobs of Americans by substituting cheap foreign labor that enhanced their profits. It was never sustainable for more than a few decades after WWII, because our capacity to create debt with a credible chance of serving interest and redeeming the principal is not infinite. The Globalist system unraveled in 2008 and has been living on borrowed time since. Now it is coming apart at the seams. It was not sustainable to expect we can export American jobs and wealth to China in return for their buying Treasurys to earn interest on our national debt, extracting more wealth from future generations.

Economics aside, it is a question of basic human fairness. Do we want an American worker who loses his or her job to imports from a country like China to have to pull his children out of college, so the Chinese owner of the factory that exports to the United States can send his or her children to American universities? Common sense suggests a country will decay when one group of citizens is betraying another group. In those circumstances, the country will be in conflict until one side subdues the other, hopefully through a constitutional political process rather than civil war. In the recent election, the side that has suffered from detrimental trade has elected a president that promised to reduce it with tariffs.

Trump's tariffs are estimated (when December's numbers are reported to fill out the year) to reduce the trade deficit with China from $295 billion in 2024 to $206 billion in 2025; the deficit with the E.U. from $235 billion to $223 billion; the deficit with Mexico increased from $171 billion to $199 billion; deficit with Vietnam will increase from $123 billion to $176 billion; with Japan a decrease from $68 billion to $63 billion; with South Korea from $66 billion to $55 billion; with India will increase from $44 billion to $58 billion, this despite tariffs of 50% (penalty for buying Russian oil) for much of the year. The trade deficit remained the same, but redistributed away from China and into Mexico, Vietnam, and India.

This is not the reduction in the trade deficit the friends of tariffs wanted, but neither was it a continuation of the rapid increases of prior years, and at least a redistribution away from China and into Mexico and Vietnam Mexico at least is a neighbor whose supply chains are on the order side of a 2,000 mile border instead of a 7,000 mile ocean, and Vietnam is a country whose prosperity we should encourage, given our intervention in their war, especially if they can be induced to buy more from us.

The GDP Deficit

The trade deficit is also a GDP deficit, because the money sent out of the country to purchase goods and services abroad is a deficit in our production of goods and services here. GDP is usually defined as Consumption + Government Spending + Investments + Balance of Trade. Consumption is the value of products at their last point of sale. Government spending is its personnel and public expenses, not including transfer programs like Social Security. Investment is the money business invests in expanding its operations. Balance of Trade is exports minus imports. Imports are subtracted from our GDP because they increase consumption but do not add production value to the economy as domestic production does.

The friends of free trade say that the subtraction of nearly a $trillion of trade deficits from our GDP each year can be misleading, because imports allow us to reallocate our production resources to higher-value products and because the US dollars foreign producers earn must return to the U.S. as investments. The part about imports allowing us to reallocate our resources to higher values of production can be partially true; but also partially false, because when industries move overseas, we rarely replace them with industries of equal value, while we incur tax burdens of paying government support for American workers who lose their jobs.

As mentioned, the part about dollars coming back to the United States is not necessarily true, since dollars can be spent anywhere in the world, not just here. A dollar that leaves the U.S, either as currency or electronically, can cycle around the world forever without returning to the U.S. Even if it comes back, it may be invested in buying real estate or inflating the stock market that does not add anything of substance to the economy that was not already there; it merely transferred the value of the work that used to be done here into a foreigners' account who used it to inflate prices of American assets, thereby harming workers twice by costing them their jobs and their ability to afford housing.

Thus, it is a good intuition that imports exceeding exports is a drag on the economy. It's why most countries encourage exports and discourage imports, and the reason NAFTA was sold to the public, presidents, and Congress on the false promise that it would create a trade surplus for the U.S.

Since 2000, we've sent $14 trillion out of this country in trade deficits, about half the $30 trillion in national debt we've run up during those 25 years. The numbers for 2023 and 2024 are:

USA GDP in 2023 was $28.3 trillion

USA GDP in 2024 was $29.7 trillion

USA GDP growth in 2024 was $1.4 trillion

Federal government tax receipts in 2024 were: $4.92 trillion

Federal government expenses in 2024 were: $6.75 trillion

Federal government deficit in 2024 was $1.83 trillion

Our GDP growth in 2024 of $1.4 trillion was $430 billion less than our growth in federal government debt of $1.83 billion. If the $918 billion trade deficit was reshored to the U.S. to bolster our GDP, our economy would have grown $488 billion more than the debt. The trade deficit is the difference between economic growth and decay.

Since 2000, our GDP has grown by $19.45 billion, from $10.25 billion in 2000 to $29.7 trillion in 2024. Since 2000, our national debt has grown by $30.46 trillion, from $5.65 trillion in 2000 to $36.13 trillion at the end of 2024. Our national debt is growing 1.57 times as much as our GDP. This will end with hyperinflation to cancel the debt, a flat-out default, or some of each.

Yes, it is entirely true that the profligate spending of Congress (both parties) accounted for the other half of the national debt, so we can't hang it all on the trade deficit. But what if we had kept that $14 trillion in the country, growing the economy, and compounding itself with dividends and growth in employment, wages, and taxes to fund the government the right way? Wouldn't our national debt be close to zero now?

In the 24 years prior to 2000, our economy grew 3.45% compounded. In the 24 years after 2000, it grew 2.16% compounded, because we were shipping the economy overseas almost as fast as we were growing it. Furthermore, we are losing our predominance in the world's economy. The USA produces 16% of the world's manufacturing GDP and China 32%, the reverse ratio of just 15 years ago. How long can the USA remain on top if that ratio continues to decline to 6% and 42% in the next 15 years? Can we trust a dodgy stock market and an increasingly shaky debt-ridden government to fund our imports?

China has become the world's most important trading country, with most countries doing more business with them than with us, even most in our hemisphere, another reversal of roles in world trade leadership between us and China as our export markets are being choked by China's industries financed with our trade deficits. The map below shows the switch in trade dominance between the USA and China since 2000. Countries in blue trade more with us than China; those in red trade more with China. There is a lot more red than blue on the 2024 map:

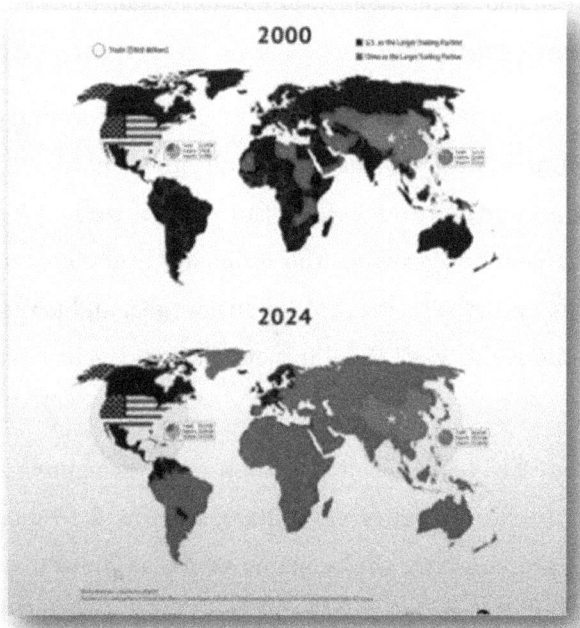

If this trend is not reversed, in another 15 years, the USA will account for 6% of the world's manufacturing and China 48%. Can any country prevail in peace or war against an adversary that outproduces it 8-to-1?

The tax deficit

Domestic products are taxed at every stage of production, from the time the raw materials are pulled out of the ground, to machining the parts, to assembly, to distribution, to retail sale --- all the value added by workers' wages, managements' compensation, company profit, and dividends to investors, plus all of those things created in the supply chains, is taxed. If a product made in the USA is sold in the USA, the $100 value has been taxed.

If a product made abroad is imported into the United States for $60 and sold by the importer to a consumer for $100, only the $40 of mark up is taxed by the United States, the other $60 having been taxed by the producing country. For that reason, other countries impose VATs on domestic and foreign companies, such that when a product is imported from a foreign country, the VAT is applied on the $60 as well as the $40. The United States does have state and local sales taxes charged at retail point of sale, but these are typically 6% to 8%, whereas VATs are typically around 20% applied to all imports, while the retail sale tax is not levied on products used in intermediate stages of production and distribution, only on products sold to the public. A tariff is a VAT on the value of imports that would otherwise not be taxed at the national level.

International trade lets companies produce in countries that don't tax exports and sell into countries that don't levy VATs, thus extracting tax-free profits. For example, Ireland does not charge corporate income or VAT taxes on products exported to other countries. An American company can move production to Ireland and export to the United States, paying taxes neither in Ireland or the United States. A great deal of money laundering is done to make Ireland look like the origin of products sold in the United States. Prior to 2017, this did not matter as much, since overseas profits were taxed when they were repatriated to the U.S. The Tax Cuts and Jobs Act of 2017 made repatriated profits tax-exempt, so American companies can produce overseas and sell in the U.S. without paying taxes when they bring the money home.

In the first 11 months of 2025, Ireland's people and businesses purchased $17.5 billon of goods and services from the United States, while American companies in Ireland exported $130 billion of untaxed products to the United States, resulting in $112 billion trade deficit. Trump's 15% tariff on imports from Ireland seems to have reduced the trade imbalance in recent months as American companies return production to the United States to avoid the tariff. Now that they are producing more in the USA, they are paying a fair share of taxes to the USA, the same as an American company that produces in the USA would.

Paying a fair share of taxes to the country where profits are earned is the principle behind VATs and tariffs. It is true that VATs are applied to a country's domestic productions as well as what it imports from abroad, but how a country taxes its domestic productions is no business of ours. We only need to care about taxing imports from other countries to about the same extent as we tax our domestic productions, and to about the same extent as they tax our exports to them.

Our tax deficit resulting from the trade deficit is added to the national debt that must be funded with the taxes of the future. Thus, we are using trade to bolster standards of living for the living, while loading the debt burden on the backs of the unborn. Our trade deficit in goods and service has increased from $381 billion in 2000 to $918 billion in 2024. Over those 24 years, the accumulated trade deficit is $14 trillion dollars, about half of our increase in the national debt.

The friends of free trade claim there is no *direct, provable* link between the trade deficit and the federal spending deficit, because the federal spending deficit would end if Presidents and Congresses would rein in spending. They are entirely right that irresponsible spending more than tax revenue is the direct cause of the government's escalating debt. After all, countries that run trade surpluses, like Japan and those in the European Union, also float their economies on oceans of debt, the same as us, and in some cases more so. Those other countries impose VAT taxes on imports as well as domestic products, so they are taxing the full value of everything sold in their countries, domestic and foreign. Now our tariffs are ginning $370 billion tax revenue on the importation of foreign product.

Tariffs bolster tax revenues either by taxing imports or by encouraging products sold in the United States to be produced here, such that the value of workers' wages, corporation profits, and corporation dividends paid to investors are taxed. Tariffs are thus revenue enhancers, whether they are levied on imports or whether they bolster domestic production. It may be true, as Libertarians are prone to say, that our government will continue to spend money in excess of tax revenues no matter how much revenue tariffs bring in, so tariffs merely increase government spending without reducing the deficit, and in that regard, they waste economic resources by taking money away from the private sector.

Since there is merit on both sides of this argument, let's consider how the trade deficit as a deficit in Americans' livelihoods.

The Labor Substitution Deficit

Free-traders do not, and apparently dare not, face the plain truth—which is that the lowest priced fabric means the lowest priced labor.

So wrote James Blaine in 1884. Free trade is supposed to be based on the theory of comparative advantage, but does that include cheap labor? The friends of free trade are loath to admit that jobs lave the United States because workers in China, Mexico, and now Vietnam, earn 90% less than Americans. This troubles both political parties, because they are funded by corporation owners who don't care about voters who suffer from detrimental trade, but the parties depend on voters to elect their politicians.

For Liberals, admitting that trade with low-wage countries devalues the livelihoods "of America's working families" undermines their pretense of caring about people of modest means. For corporation-funded Conservatives, it undermines their notion that companies move jobs overseas because "foreigners work harder than lazy Americans." Maybe foreigners in poverty-ridden countries work harder than Americans, because the alternative is starvation. But that's not why American companies move the work there. They move it there because they can hire ten foreigners for every American worker they let go. They do not have to invest in improving productivity of their American workers, when they can lay them off and move the work to other countries.

Free traders do not like to be reminded of Americans eking out lives of despair amid the ruins of de-industrialized cities and factory towns whose jobs were moved to Mexico and China turns trade into an eyesore instead of a shining engine of cutting-edge prosperity. They don't want to admit that companies profiteer by inflicting poverty on American families, so the company can inflate its profit by importing what used to be made here. This goes against the grain of conservative thinking that business can do no wrong.

Free traders among Liberals and Conservatives stand united on the common propaganda ground that "no manufacturing jobs have been lost to trade, only to robots and automation." To hear them tell it, Mexico and China are filled with legions of robots cranking out cornucopias of products with nary a human being in sight --- there are no Chinese dormitories crammed with overstressed workers jumping out the windows when pushed past their breaking points from overwork and low pay; or tens of thousands of Mexicans living in shacktowns around American-owned factories.

According to free traders, American companies move millions of jobs to Mexico and China because those are the only countries that have robots; that China is full of "dark factories" where only robots work without human supervision. The truth is that companies move American jobs to cheap-labor counties to *avoid* investing in robots and automation. What will company management do when given a choice of:

A) Spending $25,000,000 to modernize an American factory so 1,000 American workers earning $25 / hour (wages, benefits, employer-taxes) can be more productive.

B) Firing the 1,000 American workers at $25 / hour, hiring 10,000 Mexicans or Chinese at $4 / hour, and pocketing the $25,000,000 as executive bonuses and stock buybacks for the investors.

The answer is easily discoverable:

Mon, Apr 17, 2017 Boeing to lay off hundreds more engineers:

Dec 17, 2018 Boeing sets new US$20B buyback plan, raises dividend 20%

Caterpillar Inc. announced Friday it will move production of oil pumps and valves from its plant in Joliet to its facilities near Monterrey, Mexico, resulting in the loss of about 230 full-time jobs from Joliet. "The company has since completed all analysis and determined (that) to remain cost competitive it must move forward with the transition..." Caterpillar's statement said.

Microsoft unveils $17.5B India bet after 2025 US layoffs

There can be no argument with companies creating jobs in countries where profits are earned; only when they lay off American employees to move the work to other countries to make product that will be exported back to the United States; for example, U.S. auto companies exporting substantially all of the motor vehicles made by 560,000 workers in Mexico to the United States, while selling few to Mexicans, who mostly buy Japanese, South Korean, and Chinese brands.

When this reality becomes impossible to deny, free traders may admit that American jobs go to Mexico and China, but claim it is because Mexicans and Chinese "do work that Americans don't want." They pretend to forget that Americans **were** doing this work until American companies laid them off and moved their jobs out of the country. Their next fallback is claiming foreigners "have a better work ethic" than Americans, which is true, because if they don't work to maximum exertion, they and their families starve. The United States has a high standard of living because American workers don't have to work excessive hours to eke out enough to live in a tarpaper shacktown with open sewers in the streets, or to labor for months without pay on a farm until the owner sells the harvest and then decides what to pay you. How

90

far down the food chain of cheap labor should we go? Should we buy product from countries with concentration camps that work prisoners to death in factories, if those products are cheaper than what we can produce with paid labor in the USA?

American companies desire free trade treaties to mask their motive of moving American jobs out of the country because they are seeking labor substitution markets to get rid of their American workers, not common markets to promote exports that employ American workers in the United States.

The American Family Deficit

In April 2025, *The Wall Street Journal* claimed free trade had prospered Americans because:

U.S. household net worth at the end of 1999: $41 trillion. End of 2024: $160 trillion.

Here's some color on that $160 trillion of household wealth:

https://www.federalreserve.gov/releases/z1/dataviz/dfa/distribute/chart/

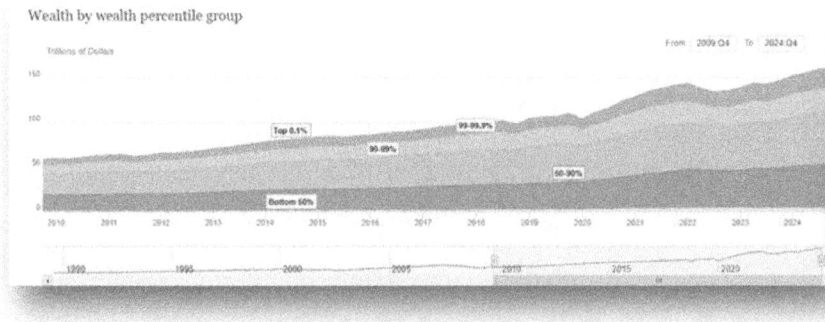

The top 1% off American families own $49 trillion of family wealth = 31% of total

The top 10% own $108 trillion =67% of the total

The top 50% own $157 trillion = 97.5% of the total

The bottom 50% own $4.10 Trillion. = 2.5% of the total.

Half of Americans gained little to nothing in those 24 years of our borders open to foreign trade. The trade deficits and job losses devalued the incomes and wealth of tens of millions of wage earners, while concentrating wealth in the top 10% of asset owners. This maldistribution of wealth has spawned discontent and possible political radicalization among our people. We have increased the national debt by

$30 trillion since 2000 trying to prop up the declining wealth of half our people, many put out of work by labor substitution trade.

Besides the dollars and cents of economics, countries must have stable societies. They become destabilized and prone to radicalism and socialist or fascist revolution when too many people lose their opportunities for gainful employment to feed and shelter themselves and their families. Advocates for laissez faire trade never seem to consider the social stabilization work provides, as opposed to people roving the streets indolent and hungry.

Are Imports Really Cheaper?

The friends of free trade say imports add value to our economy because they are cheaper than American-made products and thereby allow us to:

A) Increase our consumption.

B) Keep our consumption the same, while having surplus money to grow our wealth by investing in emerging technologies.

They are reluctant to admit that some imports may be cheap because they are lower in quality than more durable USA-made products and therefore more costly when the cost of replacement is factored. Companies do not import products to sell them cheap; only to make them cheap abroad and sell them here at inflated markups to increase their profit margins. If imported products wear out quickly and must be replaced, that is a further augmentation of their profits.

How many people have had to redo home renovations because the materials the contractor used --- or that do-it-yourselfer bought from home improvement stores --- were imported from China: screws that rusted and window trim that disintegrated   because the interior was cardboard. The contractor used the cheapest materials because it inflated his profit margins, not because he wanted to give the homeowner a bargain. The project became three times more expensive when it had to be redone with quality materials. Or how about the lawnmower blades that don't hold their edge and chew the lawn instead of cutting it. Or the Chinese cemetery monuments that crack after a year in the weather? Or the toxic Chinese pet food? Or the Chinese drywall? Or the made-in-Mexico Washing machines that last four years instead of the American-made standard of fifteen?

The few quality products made from low-wage countries, like iPhones, are sold at high prices, the same as if they were made in the USA. How many times did we hear, "If iPhones were made in the USA, they'd cost a thousand dollars, and Americans will not pay that much." Now Americans are paying that much, at least for the newest top line iPhones. Companies always sell at the highest price that will maximize their profits. Just because a product is made with cheap labor doesn't mean it will be sold cheaply in the U.S.

Are Imports the Consumers' Choice?

The friends of free trade play up the Libertarian angle that imports are purchased because people want them. But when were we asked if we wanted to buy imports? We buy what the retailers stock the shelves with, and if 97% of the products are from China (as was once alleged with our largest retailer) that's what we buy. If every seafood item in the grocery store is processed in China, and we want seafood, what are we going to buy? If the restaurant on the fishing peer buys its seafood from China instead of the commercial fishing pier, who is going to know? Retailers and restaurants stock their inventories with imports to inflate their profit margins, not because consumers want them.

It's like the ethanol mandate for gasoline. Nobody would voluntarily purchase gasoline with ethanol. The few gas stations that offer ethanol-free gasoline have long lines of people queued up at the no-ethanol pump. People are forced to buy gasoline with ethanol they don't want because a few agribusiness companies wanted to profiteer by building refineries converting corn to ethanol paid Senators and Congresspersons to enact legislation forcing consumers to buy it. 99.9% of the people are suffering for the benefit of the .1% who bribed Congress.

Companies likewise force imports on the public, because they, not consumers, decide what is sold to the public.

"All Are Better than Either"

During the Civil War, Abraham Lincoln said the country could not be divided without damaging all its people:

And this is true, wherever a dividing or boundary line may be fixed. Place it between the now free and slave country, or place it south of Kentucky or north of Ohio, and still the truth remains that none south of it can trade to any port or place north of it, and none north of it can trade to any port or place south of it, except upon terms dictated by a government foreign to them. These outlets, east, west, and south, are indispensable to the well-being of the people inhabiting and to inhabit this vast interior region. Which of the three may be the best is no proper question. All are better than either, and all of right belong to that people and to their successors forever.

Lincoln, Abraham. The Writings of Abraham Lincoln.

Today, the Free Trade Mavens are attempting to divide the nation along economic lines, claiming that industry is obsolete, while agriculture and technology must be cherished. We must tell them, as Mr. Lincoln told his cohorts, that "All are better than either."

INDUSTRY, AGRICULTURE, and TECHNOLOGY:

WHICH OF THE THREE MAY BE THE BEST
IS NO PROPER QUESTION.
ALL ARE BETTER THAN EITHER, AND ALL OF
RIGHT BELONG TO THAT PEOPLE AND TO THEIR SUCCESSORS

Industry vs. Agriculture

Let's recall Adam Smith's words from **The Wealth of Nations:**

The most opulent nations, indeed, generally excel all their neighbors in agriculture as well as in manufactures; but they are commonly more distinguished by their superiority in the latter than in the former.

Today's friends of free trade hold a dimmer view of their Founding Father's dogma. Their heroes are no longer the Captains of Industry like Henry Ford, who created the wheels of American industrial prosperity, or Walter Reauther, the happy warrior for workers ho reminded Mr. Ford that if he wanted to sell his cars, he had to pay his workers enough to buy them. Their new paladin springs from the Earth full blown as Judge Soy Bean, the new ruler of the Free Trade Maven economy, as **The Wall Street Journal** reports:

Trump Bets the Soybean Farm on Tariffs

The damage from the trade war turns out to be mutually assured.

By The Editorial Board Follow
Sept. 29, 2025 5:43 pm ET

⌲ ▢ AA ▢ 741 ⊘ Gift unlocked article   ⌂ Listen (3 min) ⋮

Soybeans are harvested in Warren, Ind. MICHAEL CONROY/ASSOCIATED PRESS

Whoever claimed trade wars are easy to win clearly wasn't an American farmer. Witness the enormous collateral damage America's soybean producers are suffering amid President Trump's trade war with China.

Exports of American soybeans to China have collapsed this year, with no new orders logged in recent months ahead of the prime autumn export season. Before Mr. Trump's first round of tariffs on China in 2018, China was the largest export market for American soy. It typically bought about 30% of total U.S. soybean production and some 60% of American soybean exports. Those exports were worth $12.8 billion annually, the soybean farmers' trade association reports.

Free Trade Mavens believe $12.8 billion of soybean commodity exports to China are worth more than the $half trillion of manufactured product we imported from China every year until Trump clamped down on it. And the $3 trillion of debt we incurred floating our locked-down economy when the Chinese government spread COVID around the world instead of quarantining it. It would take 234 years of soybean exports to China to pay for that --- almost as many years since we signed the Declaration of Independence. According to Free Trade Mavens, Trump's tariffs on Chinese product are in the same league as other crises of American history, including the firing on Fort Sumter that ignited the Civil War, killing over 600,000 Americans:

So Much Trade Losing

The tariff shooting begins with China, and where's the deal-making?

By The Editorial Board [Follow]

July 6, 2018 6:38 pm E T

↪ ⊓ aA ⬚ 469   ⌀ Gift unlocked article

Soybeans are loaded into a truck after being harvested at the Santa Cruz farm near Atibaia, Brazil.
PATRICIA MONTEIRO/BLOOMBERG NEWS

So much Trade Losing:

The tariff shooting begins with China, and where's the deal-making?

By The Editorial Board July 6, 2018

The shooting has begun in the U.S.-China trade war, and let's hope it's not Fort Sumter. *The South figured the Civil War would last a few weeks, but things happened. That's the nature of trade wars as well, and while no one is likely to win this confrontation, both sides could certainly lose.*

Early Friday the U.S. followed through on President Trump's threats by imposing tariffs of 25% on $34 billion of Chinese imports, and Beijing retaliated on an equal value of U.S. goods. Those amounts are too small to tank either economy, but trade talks have stalled, meaning more tariffs could come as soon as next month.

The damage is already serious for American soybean farmers whose biggest customer is China.

Free Trade Mavens believe agriculture is superior to manufacturing, such that we can ship millions of industrial jobs and $trillions of industrial productions out of the country without incurring detrimental consequences, but the economy will fail when China tariffs $10 billion of our soybeans because we tariffed $500 billion of their exports to us. In fact, the Chinese are not buying our soybeans because it is a commodity in surplus on world markets, and they can buy them cheaper from Brazil.

What motivates the Free Trade Mavens to denigrate American industry as an archaic pursuit having no place in the modern USA, while worshiping the soybean, that saw the first light of day 6,000 years ago in China? They frame farming as the pinnacle of American business prowess and telling us we need millions of indigent foreigners to crawl the muddy fields on their hands and knees, picking root crops the same as their early Cro Magnon ancestors did it 50,000 years ago. But they say anything having to do with manufacturing is archaic and must be handed off to cheap labor countries.

Perhaps it is because trade allows Wall Street money funds to buy American industrial companies and ship their production equipment overseas to be manned by cheap labor, but they haven't figured out to ship a farm with a million tons of dirt overseas, so they protect that business by importing millions of foreign laborers here to yank the fruit from the orchards on rickety ladders and paw the root crops from the mud with their hands. Free Trade Mavens who claim industrial jobs must be moved overseas because only Third World countries like China and Mexico have robots and automation, invent copious excuses to explain why farming cannot be automated after 8,000 years, and requires the indigent and ignorant labor of the world to be brought into the U.S. to bring in the harvest.

Free Trade Mavens are not looking for common markets to sell American exports, but for labor substitution markets to produce at the lowest cost and import into the United States to sell at the highest markups. They never talk about robots reducing labor in farming, because they only care about the $4 / hour labor. They talk about farming as if crops were golden nuggets leached from our priceless soil by the turnip-stained hands of toiling millions of indigent foreigners, while industrial plants built with $billions of capital investment should be shuttered and thousands of well-paying jobs by skilled American workers obliterated. They cling to those turnips, taters, and especially soybeans as if they were diamonds in the rough.

They need to consider that the 99.6% of the economy that isn't soybeans has value too:

1) Today we have 16% of the world's manufacturing capacity. China has 32%. 15 years ago those proportions were reversed.

2) Our inflation-adjusted manufacturing value peaked in inflation-adjusted value in December 2007

3) In the 24 years before 2000, the year we opened the borders to unfettered imports from China by letting them into the World Trade

Organization, our GDP grew 3.45% compounded. After 2000 it fell to 2.16% compounded.

4) While our GDP grew 2.16% after 2000, our national debt grew 6.65% compounded.

5) The increases in national debt from 2000 to 2024 was $30 trillion. The accumulated trade deficit was $14 trillion.

6) Last year the GDP grew $1.4 trillion. The national debt grew $1.83 trillion. The trade deficit in goods and services was $918 billion. GDP growth less federal debt growth is negative since 2000.

Free Trade Mavens have divorced the industry that made us a world power and wedded their economic natures to Judge Soy Bean, a marriage made in Purgatory:

Industry vs. Technology

If the soybean can't become the new gold standard that holds up our economy when industry is offshored, perhaps technology will do it. Maybe we can become a purely technology driven economy where AI does all the work. The deficiency in this theory is that technology is sterile unless there is something to technologize. We require housing, transportation vehicles, clothing, furniture, appliances, and recreational products, and much else to elevate our lives above the caves. Technology can plan forecast the demand and plan the distribution of these products, but they still must be manufactured.

And suppose the day comes when all this can be done without human beings? We still must tax the value of production, and distribute the money for humans, otherwise no human will have money to purchase the robots' production. If the production is all done overseas, it will have to be taxed to pay Americans to buy it. But why would we want to import the product from distant countries, when it can just as well be produced here, even if by robots?

Tariffs

Country	Tariffs Charged to the U.S.A.	U.S.A. Discounted Reciprocal Tariffs	Country	Tariffs Charged to the U.S.A.	U.S.A. Discounted Reciprocal Tariffs
China	67%	34%	Peru	30%	10%
European Union	39%	20%	Nicaragua	36%	18%
Vietnam	66%	20%	Norway	75%	10%
Taiwan	64%	20%	Costa Rica	10%	10%
Japan	59%	22%	Jordan	10%	10%
India	52%	26%	Dominican Republic	10%	10%
South Korea	52%	22%	United Arab Emirates	20%	10%
Thailand	61%	32%	New Zealand	20%	20%
Switzerland	61%	32%	Argentina	20%	10%
Indonesia	64%	32%	Ecuador	10%	10%
Malaysia	61%	32%	Guatemala	10%	10%
United Kingdom	47%	32%	Honduras	10%	10%
South Africa	52%	38%	Madagascar	27%	47%
Brazil	59%	22%	Myanmar (Burma)	27%	28%
Bangladesh	61%	32%	Tunisia	20%	20%
Singapore	60%	30%	Kazakhstan	20%	37%
Israel	61%	22%	Serbia	10%	37%
Philippines	47%	10%	Egypt	10%	10%
Chile	50%	26%	Saudi Arabia	27%	22%
Australia	50%	24%	El Salvador	20%	29%
Pakistan	50%	24%	Côte d'Ivoire	20%	29%
Turkey	10%	10%	Laos	10%	10%
Colombia	10%	10%	Trinidad and Tobago	120%	10%

"Tariff" has an archaic sound, like some other old English words life "sheriff" that conjure up those ancient days of every town protecting itself from competition with products from two towns over. Part of the impetus of the United States to revolt against the British Empire, then organize our Constitution Government, was the desire for tariff-free trade among ourselves and where appropriate with the rest of the world --- like democracy, a novel idea:

At the close of the eighteenth century the barbarous superstitions of the Middle Ages concerning trade between nations still flourished with scarcely diminished vitality. The epoch-making work of Adam Smith had been published in the same year in which the United States declared their independence. The one was the great scientific event, as the other was the great political event of the age; but of neither the one nor the other were the scope and purport fathomed at the time.

The simple principle that when two parties trade. both must be gainers, or one would soon stop trading, was generally lost sight of; and most commercial legislation proceeded upon the theory that in trade, as in gambling or betting, what the one party gains the other must lose. Hence towns, districts, and nations surrounded themselves with walls of legislative restrictions intended to keep out the monster Trade, or to admit him only on strictest proof that he could do no harm.

Meanwhile, the different states, with their different tariff and tonnage acts, began to make commercial war upon one another. No sooner had the other three New England states virtually closed their ports to British shipping than Connecticut threw hers wide open, an act which she followed up by laying duties upon imports from Massachusetts. Pennsylvania discriminated against Delaware, and New Jersey, pillaged at once by both her greater neighbors, was compared to a cask tapped at both ends. The conduct of New York became especially selfish and blameworthy.

Late in 1785, when the Virginia legislature had wrangled itself into imbecility over the question of clothing Congress with power over trade, Madison hit upon an expedient. He prepared a motion to the effect that commissioners from all the states should hold a meeting, and discuss the best method of securing a uniform treatment of commercial questions;

Fiske, John, The Critical Period of American History 1783-1789. Evergreen Review, Inc. Kindle Edition.

Those talks of commercial harmony among the quasi-sovereign states of the Articles of Confederation government spawned the Constitution Convention unifying the states under a superior federal government that harmonized the trade between them. When the continuity of the federal government was threatened by the Civil War,

President Lincoln again appeal to trade as a necessary unifying principle:

...but separate our common country into two nations, as designed by the present rebellion, and every man of this great interior region is thereby cut off from some one or more of these outlets, not perhaps by a physical barrier, but by embarrassing and onerous trade regulations.

Yet, as soon as the Constitution was ratified, the very first act of the new government was the Tariff Act of 1789. And Mr. Lincoln remained a lifelong friend of modest tariffs, so long as they raised revenue for the national government and were reasonably fair to all classes of people in all parts of the country:

The object of the meeting was stated by Mr. Lincoln of Springfield, who offered the following resolutions, which were unanimously adopted: Resolved, That a tariff of duties on imported goods, producing sufficient revenue for the payment of the necessary expenditures of the National Government, and so adjusted as to protect American industry, is indispensably necessary to the prosperity of the American people. Resolved, That we are opposed to direct taxation for the support of the National Government.

Years later, just before the onset of the Civil War, he recited the tariff plank platform he'd been elected on:

"That, while providing revenue for the support of the General Government by duties upon imports, sound policy requires such an adjustment of these imposts as will encourage the development of the industrial interest of the whole country; and we commend that policy of national exchanges which secures to working-men liberal wages, to agriculture remunerating prices, to mechanics and manufacturers

adequate return for their skill, labor, and enterprise, and to the nation commercial prosperity and independence."

As with all general propositions, doubtless, there will be shades of difference in construing this. I have by no means a thoroughly matured judgment upon this subject, especially as to details; some general ideas are about all.

The eternal tariff question, then as now, is whether if it be true that tariff-free trade between the states is the engine of United States prosperity, then why would it be untrue that tariff-free trade with all the nations of the earth should not improve the engine? Proponents of tariffs must answer that question if they want their position to prevail in the public mind.

Tariffs as a Founding Principle

The Tariff Act of 1789 was the first act of the first United States Congress after the ratification of the Constitution and signed into law by President George Washington. That first tariff was purposed to raise revenue to operate the federal government and pay off its Revolutionary War debt. Secretary of the Treasury Alexander Hamilton reiterated the importance of tariffs to bolster the United States economy with manufacturing:

Hamilton's Report on Manufacturers, December 5, 1791

The expediency of encouraging manufactures in the United States...appears at this time to be pretty generally admitted.

The employment of machinery forms an item of great importance in the general mass of national industry...if it is the interest of the United

States to open every possible avenue to emigration from abroad, it affords a weighty argument for the encouragement of manufactures...

There seems to be a moral certainty that the trade of a country which is both manufacturing and agricultural will be more lucrative and prosperous than that of a country which is, merely agricultural. . . .

Not only the wealth, but the independence and security of a country, appear to be materially connected with the prosperity of manufactures. Every nation, with a view to those great objects, ought to endeavor to possess within itself all the essentials of national supply.

Hamilton believed the United States could not become strong unless we developed an industrial base capable of producing most of what we consume. Even at that early date his proposed tariffs were opposed by Southerners who preferred to import cheaper tariff-free merchandise from Britain. Thomas Jefferson saw tariffs as an incubator of the industrial workers he distrusted:

Those who labor in the earth are the chosen people of God...let us never wish to see our citizens occupied at a workbench or twirling a distaff.

For the general operations of manufacture, let our workshops remain in Europe. It is better to carry provisions and materials to workmen there, than bring them to the provisions and materials, and with them their manners and principles. The loss by the transportation of commodities across the Atlantic will be made up in happiness and permanence of government.

The mobs of great cities add just so much to the support of pure government, as sores do to the strength of the human body. A degeneracy in these is a canker which soon eats to the heart of its laws and constitution.

This set the United States on the course of dividing into the agricultural South and the commercial North. We might have become two nations if our first President George Washington had not mediated the dispute, siding with Hamilton. Washington's wise words could be applied today when either side of the debate becomes hyperbolic:

Mankind cannot think alike but would adopt different means to attain the same end. For I will frankly and solemnly declare that I believe the views of both of you are pure and well meant; and that experience alone will decide with respect to the salubrity of the measures which are the subjects of dispute.

Washington calmed the tariff feud between Hamilton and Jefferson, but it resurfaced decades later during the Nullification Crisis of 1832-1833 when South Carolina's state government threatened to prevent, the federal government's customs agents from collecting the so-called "Tariff of Abominations" on foreign trade through South Carolina ports. South Carolina's defiant "Nullifiers" backed down when President Andrew Jackson threatened to march a national army into the state and hang the Nullifiers "higher than Haman (a Biblical miscreant)." President Jackson wrote, "The tariff was only a pretext, and disunion and southern confederacy the real object. The next pretext will be the negro, or slavery question."

Abraham Lincoln applied his wisdom to the tariff question as he rose to national prominence, from the 1840s until the Civil War, discussing it in about the same way it is discussed today:

Several resolutions were adopted by the meeting.... The first declares a tariff of duties upon foreign importations, producing sufficient revenue for the support of the General Government, and so adjusted as to protect American industry, to be indispensably necessary to the prosperity of the American people....

"To be independent for the comforts of life, we must fabricate them ourselves. We must now place the manufacturer by the side of the agriculturalist. The grand inquiry now is, Shall we make our own comforts, or go without them at the will of a foreign nation? He, therefore, who is now against domestic manufactures must be for reducing us to dependence on foreign nations.

The question of revenue we will now briefly consider. For several years, the revenues of the government have been unequal to its expenditures, and consequently loan after loan, sometimes direct and sometimes indirect in form, has been resorted to.

By this means, a new national debt has been created and is still growing on us with a rapidity fearful to contemplate --- a rapidity only reasonably to be expected in time of war. This state of things has been produced by a prevailing unwillingness either to increase the tariff or resort to direct taxation [income tax]. But the one or the other must come. Coming expenditures must be met, and the present debt must be paid; and money cannot always be borrowed for these objects. The system of loans is but temporary in its nature and must soon explode.

It is a system not only ruinous while it lasts, but one that must soon fail and leave us destitute. As an individual who undertakes to live by borrowing soon finds his original means devoured by interest, and, next, no one left to borrow from, so must it be with a government.

We repeat, then, that a tariff sufficient for revenue, or a direct tax, must soon be resorted to; and, indeed, we believe this alternative is now denied by no one.

Let us, then, briefly compare the two systems. The tariff is the cheaper system, because the duties, being collected in large parcels at a few commercial points, will require comparatively few officers in their collection; while by the direct-tax system the land must be literally covered with assessors and collectors, going forth like swarms of Egyptian locusts, devouring every blade of grass and other green thing. And, again, by the tariff system the whole revenue is paid by the consumers of foreign goods, and those chiefly the luxuries, and not the necessaries, of life.

By this system the man who contents himself to live upon the products of his own country pays nothing at all. And surely that country is extensive enough, and its products abundant and varied enough, to answer all the real wants of its people. In short, by this system the burden of revenue falls almost entirely on the wealthy and luxurious few, while the substantial and laboring many who live at home, and upon home products, go entirely free.

By the direct-tax system no one can escape. However strictly the citizen may exclude from his premises all foreign luxuries --- fine cloths, fine silks, rich wines, golden chains, and diamond rings --- -still, for the possession of his house, his barn, and his homespun, he is to be perpetually haunted and harassed by the tax-gatherer. With these views we leave it to be determined whether we or our opponents are the more truly democratic on the subject.

It is often said that the tariff is the specialty of Pennsylvania [speaking in Pittsburgh]. Assuming that direct taxation is not to be adopted, the tariff question must be as durable as the government itself. So far there is little difference of opinion among the people. It is as to whether, and how far, duties on imports shall be adjusted to favor home production in the home market, that controversy begins. One party insists that such adjustment oppresses one class for the advantage of another; while the other party argues that, with all its incidents, in the long run all classes are benefited.

Permit me, fellow-citizens, to read the tariff plank of the Chicago [Republican Party] platform, or rather have it read in your hearing by one who has younger eyes.

That, while providing revenue for the support of the General Government by duties upon imports, sound policy requires such an adjustment of these imposts as will encourage the development of the industrial interest of the whole country; and we commend that policy of national exchanges which secures to working-men liberal wages, to agriculture remunerating prices, to mechanics and manufacturers adequate return for their skill, labor, and enterprise, and to the nation commercial prosperity and independence.

Mr. Lincoln thought of the tariff 170 years ago the same way tariff advocates today do, to raise revenue to pay down the national debt --- thereby avoiding the alternatives of excise and income taxes levied on Americans --- while providing protection from foreign competition to our domestic industries and their employees. The purposes of raising revenue and protecting industry are somewhat at odds, because a modest tariff raises more revenue and protects domestic industry less, while a high tariff protects domestic industry but raises less revenue because imports are priced out of the market. If the tariff is high, a foreign producer desiring to sell in the United States must relocate to the United States to escape it, thereby employing American workers who pay taxes. American producers may also expand their market, thereby paying more taxes. Tariffs create tax revenue, directly if they are modest, or indirectly if high enough to incentivize more production and employment in the United States.

Though not a substantive cause of the Civil War, the tariff question may have played a role in the election of Abraham Lincoln in 1860. Pennsylvania, then as now, was the most heavily industrialized state, and Mr. Lincoln favored protecting its industries. Pennsylvania held statewide elections in October 1860 that went Republican. The results of these elections may have influenced the presidential elections in Ohio, Indiana, and Illinois in November, Mr. Lincoln narrowly winning their electoral votes by a percent or two, the same way Trump was twice elected president by the electoral votes of the Industrial Midwest.

Tariffs have stirred two other controversies since 1833. The first was the off-year Congressional elections of 1890, that caused the tariff-levying Republican Party to lose more than a third of their seats in the House of Representatives, and four in the Senate. The champion of the tariffs was Congressman William McKinley, who ran on the campaign slogan, "Bill McKinley and the McKinley (tariff) Bill!"

The Democrats repealed McKinley's Tariff in 1894. By then the economy was in an even more severe depression. The Republicans, delighting in blaming the economic catastrophe on the Democrats' repeal of tariffs, came roaring back in 1896, electing tariff champion William McKinley as president. By then, McKinley had moderated his position on tariffs, desiring them only to protect American industries that allegedly suffered unfair competition by nations such as Britain, whose governments were prone to subsidizing their industries with public money.

Fate smiled on President McKinley. Great quantities of gold were coincidentally discovered in Alaska and Canada's Yukon as soon as he was inaugurated. Since the United States minted dollars from gold, the money supply increased, creating a mild dose of beneficial inflation, allowing people to pay off their old debts, and undertake new business ventures. Our victorious war with Spain required massive government purchases of warships, military materiel, and pay for thousands of soldiers and sailors who volunteered to fight. With gold flowing into the economy, the revival of the economy was spectacular, as reported in the financial press:

- *The nation leaped at once into an era of unprecedented prosperity. As is always the case, a brilliantly successful foreign war stimulated commercial activity in every quarter...the year 1899 became an annus mirabilis in the records of American commerce and finance. Capital, which had long been locked up by its timid owners, now came forth and reaped abundant profits. All the staple products of the country were in keen demand, and prices soared almost every day.*

- *All trade reports show that our factories are taxed to their utmost capacity in filling their orders. The railroads are unable to cope with the traffic that is offered; and on every hand we hear of a record-breaking business and constantly increasing wages, the latter in many cases as much as 10 and 15 percent.*

Whether or not the imposition of tariffs, their repeal, and their modest re-imposition had much, if any, effect on the economy is hard to say, but because the economy recovered so spectacularly after McKinley was elected, the people decided the Republicans must know what they were doing, tariffs and all. The Republicans became the dominant party until 1932.

Historian Brooks Adams, grandson of our second President John Adams, noted that the quaint world of frontiersmen, quiet county seat towns on the hills and prairies, was being surpassed by roaring American industrial power of noise and energy that would remake the world:

I came home straight [on the train [from San Francisco] and sat most of the time in an observation car. Beginning on the crest of the Rockies the [renewed tide of industrial prosperity] flows down into the Mississippi Valley, and then across to the eastern mountains in an ever-increasing flood, with an ever-heightening velocity. At last you come to the Lakes and Buffalo. No one who has watched that torrent from its source on the Divide to its discharge In New York Bay can, I think, help feeling that the hour of the old world has struck.

Tariffs enjoyed their day in the sun.

The Smoot-Hawley Tariff

The Smoot-Hawley Tariff of 1930 crystalized opposition to tariffs, since it occurred against the canvas of general economic collapse during the Great Depression of 1939-1940. Thus, an understanding of this tariff is necessary for gleaning a proper view of tariffs vs. free trade.

The 1920s were prosperous as American manufacturers innovated new technologies scientific management techniques. Automobiles, radios, electrical appliances, and hundreds of other items were produced in great quantity at affordable prices. During this era of prosperity, Congress enacted tariffs averaging 40% on about 37% of the products grown or manufactured in the United States, leaving 63% un-tariffed.

Some tariffed products were commodities like wheat produced in countries exceeding what their markets could consume, thereby lowering the market price below the cost of production. Senator Reed Smoot and Congressman Willis Hawley, who wrote the tariff that bears their names, were from the agricultural and ranching states of Oregon and Utah. It was passed by Congress and signed by President Herbert hoover in June 1930, eight months after the onset of the Great Depression in late October 1929. It was a modest tariff, as recently explained in *The Wall Street Journal* by way of comparison to President Trump's 2025 tariffs:

https://www.wsj.com/economy/trade/how-global-trade-could-survive-trumps-tariffs-24d74d08

Greg Ip April 7, 2025 5:30 am ET

Trump's tariffs are a bigger economic shock than Smoot-Hawley. Back then, the U.S. was already a high-tariff country with an average duty of 36%. Smoot-Hawley raised that by just 6 percentage points, according to Doug Irwin, author of "Clashing Over Commerce: A History of U.S. Trade Policy." That grew to 19 points because tariffs were set in dollar amounts and rose in percentage terms as prices fell amid the depression.

It was an unwise increase, but not a radical break from the tariffs enacted during the prosperous 1920s, but not the trigger of the Great Depression it is frequently made out to be.

The Great Depression was triggered by real estate and stock market speculation that got out of hand as the business cycle peaked when people had all the housing, cars, radios, washing machines, and every other modern appliance they could afford. As in the prior depressions of the late 1800s --- and the future Great Recession of 2008-201 --- demand slackened, loans were called in by tottering banks, and companies laid off millions of workers. The crisis was intensified by failing banks whose capital was destroyed by playing the stock market with depositors' money, a shady banking practice repeated in 2008. By the middle of 1930s unemployment was 25% and formerly prosperous Americans were sifting food from garbage dumps. Farmers destroyed their produce because the starving unemployed did not have money. People lost their homes when they defaulted on mortgages, then the banks failed, wiping out depositors' savings because there was no federal deposit insurance in those days.

https://en.wikipedia.org/wiki/Smoot%E2%80%93Hawley_Tariff_Act

Most economists hold the opinion that the [Smoot-Hawley] tariff act did not greatly worsen the great depression:

Douglas A. Irwin writes: "most economists, both liberal and conservative, doubt that Smoot-Hawley played much of a role in the subsequent contraction. Milton Friedman also held the opinion that the Smoot-Hawley tariff of 1930 did not cause the Great Depression."[16].

According to Paul Krugman, "Protectionism was a result of the Depression, not a cause. Rising tariffs didn't even play a large role in the initial trade contraction...Where protectionism really mattered was in preventing a recovery in trade when production recovered".[17]

William Bernstein writes "most economic historians now believe that only a minuscule part of that huge loss of both world GDP and the United States' GDP can be ascribed to the tariff wars "because trade was only nine percent of global output, not enough to account for the seventeen percent drop in GDP following the Crash. He thinks the damage done could not possibly have exceeded 2 percent of world GDP and tariff "didn't even significantly deepen the Great Depression."

However, the Smoot-Hawley tariff may have expedited the rise of fascist, imperialist, and military leaders in Germany, Italy, and Japan who sought to revive the old Great Power dreams of imperial conquests to acquire continent-sized areas of Europe, the Mediterranean, and the Pacific as economic self-sufficiency areas of natural resources and captive consumer markets. The tariff certainly damaged relations between the great democracies of the United States, Canada, the United Kingdom, and France at a time when solidarity against the expansionist Axis powers was sorely needed. It put the world in an "every country for itself" mode that heightened national antagonisms leading into World War II, and for that reason alone was ill-advised.

In 1932 the Democrats swept the Republicans from office, as they'd done 40 years before in 1892. This time they had Franklin Roosevelt, of monumental stature, as their candidate. Heavily industrialized Pennsylvania again played a curious, though this time non-decisive role, by being the only large state to vote for the despised President Herbert Hoover, who the rest of the country blamed for the

Great Depression, though the fundamental causes were larger than any president's or party's politics.

President Roosevelt and the Congressional Democrats who swept into the House and Senate repealed the Smoot-Hawley and began lowering tariffs. Their method of fighting the Great Depression was to take the United States off the domestic gold standard that limited the amount of paper money the Treasury could print by requiring it be redeemable in gold bullion held in bank vaults. When the gold standard for domestic commerce was revoked in 1933, the government could print as much paper money as it needed to pump up the economy with government-funded public works projects that got the unemployed off the streets and into government-sponsored public works camps. These were inflationary dollars, but inflation was needed when the price of everything was close to zero due to people not having employment or assets of value as foundations of purchasing power. "Reflating" the economy with paper money, plus laws to rein in the banks from engaging in imprudent stock market speculations got the economy back on its feet and military production.

In the election of 1940, the Republicans, heretofore known as the party of tariffs, joined Democrats with a low-tariff policy. The Republican candidate was Wendell Wilkie, an internationalist author of One *World* urging world federalism, who served as Roosevelt's roving ambassador to maintain our wartime alliances with the Soviet Union and the British Empire.

The Smoot-Hawley Tariff was an unwise, especially increasing the tariff schedule of 40%. However, it had nothing to do with causing the Great Depression, as it was not enacted until after the economy failed due to a hyperactive business cycle with banking and stock market malfeasance. It is sometimes used as a smokescreen to cover the true causes of the Great Depression, especially to divert attention away from the irresponsible speculations with borrowed money in business, stock market, and real estate transactions, augmented by the government's lack of oversight of shady banking and stock market shenanigans. The fundamental banking reform during the Great Depression was the Glass-Steagall Act forbidding banks from playing the stock market with depositors' money. When this act was repealed by Congress in 1999, the banks promptly began engaging the same sort of reckless speculations that wrecked the economy in 1929. The bankers blew up the economy again in 2008, despite our being at the apex of the free trade era.

If free trade advocates are convinced that the "Smoot-Hawley" tariffs caused the Great Depression of 1929-1940, then they should explain why the economy also failed in the Great Recession of 2008 --- *after* we signed all those free trade deals that eliminated tariffs. The economy failed in 2008 for the same reasons as in 1929, because of reckless banking speculations at the top of a business cycle in the late 1990s when the Depression Era regulations on banks were repealed.

Smoot-Hawley should not be over-interpreted as a cause of economic distress. In the 1920s we ran trade surpluses and did not import product from cheap-labor countries used as labor substitution markets to transfer Americans' jobs out of the United States. Whereas today, we are transferring Americans' jobs and accumulated wealth to other countries because our market is open to their exports while their markets either lack wealth to buy our products if they are poor, or their governments and businesses are protectionist cartels that block our exports.

President Reagan's Selective Tariffs

Ronald Reagan was a Libertarian-minded free trade President, who said:

Our trade policy rests firmly on the foundation of free and open markets. I recognize. . . the inescapable conclusion that all of history has taught: the freer the flow of world trade, the stronger the tides of human progress and peace among nations.

Yet he saw the need for selective tariffs to help American companies, and their workers, get back on their feet, during a time when imports, mostly from Japan, were flooding the United States. American auto companies Ford, GM, and Chrysler were the hardest hit. Their troubles were self-inflicted, with bloated management and excessively paid union workers producing overcomplicated gas-hogging cars at a time when quality of manufacture was not a high priority. Over the decades, dozens of independent car companies were rolled up into the oligarchy of the Big Three of General Motors, Ford, and Chrysler, and innovation and quality left the industry. Other industries were complacent and stagnant, while the economy was weakened by a decade of high inflation caused by excessive government spending, including diversion of investment from the civil economy to the Vietnam War and the expansion of social welfare programs.

The United States had generously opened our markets to our defeated World War II enemies of Japan and Germany, while funding the reconstruction of their economies. The Japanese especially responded with vigor and wisdom, basing their return to the ranks of the world's top economic powers by understanding the American auto market better than our companies did. The Japanese brought in

American efficiency and quality control to restart their auto industry with the world's best practices. The Japanese Ministry of International Trade and Industry protected their market from imports and subsidized the Japanese auto companies, and soon there were a dozen competitive companies organized along the best manage principles and exporting to the United States the small, simple, reliable, gas-efficient cars we wanted as the cost of gasoline and auto repairs soared in the inflationary 1970s.

President Reagan decided our industries needed protection while they implemented Japanese quality control methods --- that the Japanese ironically learned from our quality gurus the Big Three ignored during the boom in peacetime production after World War II --- while Reagan's economic policies of lower taxes and regulations improved business conditions generally. He imposed tariffs and the Voluntary Export Restraints executive order limiting motor vehicles the Japanese could export to the United States. This displeased the friends of free trade, including the Libertarian Mises Institute:

https://mises.org/library/ronald-reagan-protectionist

Ronald Reagan: Protectionist

When he imposed a 100% tariff on selected Japanese electronic products for allegedly "dumping" computer memory chips, he said he did it "to enforce the principles of free and fair trade." And Treasury Secretary James A. Baker has boasted about the protectionist record: Reagan "has granted more import relief to U.S. industry than any of his predecessors in more than half a century."

The [Reagan] administration has thus far:

- *Forced Japan to accept restraints on auto exports.*

- *Tightened considerably the quotas on imported sugar.*
- *Negotiated to increase the restrictiveness of...trade in textiles and apparel.*
- *Required 18 countries, to accept "voluntary restraint agreements" that reduce their steel imports to the United States.*
- *Imposed a 45% duty on Japanese motorcycles for the benefit of Harley Davidson.*
- *Raised tariffs on Canadian lumber and cedar shingles.*
- *Forced the Japanese into an agreement to control the price of computer memory chips.*
- *Removed third-world countries on several occasions from the duty-free import program.*
- *Pressed Japan to force its automakers to buy more American-made parts.*
- *Demanded that Taiwan, West Germany, Japan, and Switzerland restrain their exports of machine tools.*
- *Accused the Japanese of dumping roller bearings.*
- *Accused the Japanese of dumping forklift trucks and color picture tubes.*
- *Extended quotas on imported clothes pins.*

Many foreign companies relocated production to the United States, bringing competition to our auto industry the Big Three needed to goad their self-improvement. Toyota, Honda, Nissan, Subaru, Mazda, Mitsubishi Kawasaki (engines), Volkswagen, BMW, Mercedes, Hyundai, and KIA were soon producing in the U.S. with high-quality management and motivated, mostly non-union workers. These factories mostly located into formerly depressed areas of the American Sunbelt, enabling millions of American workers to earn livelihoods close to their homes. Other

European companies like Airbus, Thyssen Steel, and Bayer invested here. These companies hired American workers, contracted with American components manufacturers, and produced the quality products at affordable prices Americans wanted. Those tariffs brought competition to the United States instead of sheltering it.

https://americancompass.org/the-import-quota-that-remade-the-auto-industry/

The Import Quota that Remade the Auto Industry

Executive Summary

In 1980, Japanese automakers were trouncing Detroit's "Big Three" in the American car market. After decades of intensive state support, Japanese firms had developed the world's most efficient production processes and made the highest-quality cars. Without the time and resources to retool, American automakers risked bankruptcy and mass layoffs. President Ronald Reagan negotiated a quota on Japanese imports that stemmed competition for four years, bought Detroit time to retool, and spurred massive foreign investment in a new manufacturing base in the South that created hundreds of thousands of American jobs.

Key Lessons

International economic competition defies free-market dogma. According to market fundamentalists, free markets are supposed to create incentives and competitive pressures that spur productivity and innovation. Active efforts by policymakers are supposed to backfire.

The Japanese auto industry, insulated from foreign competition and subsidized by the state, was not a catastrophic failure, but a global leader in quality and innovation. America's open market did not foster more resilient, productive, or innovative firms; it exposed them to near-

fatal import competition. Only when American policymakers stepped in did the domestic manufacturing base improve and grow.

Rather than fostering sclerosis and cronyism, the import quota encouraged innovation, spurred investment, and boosted long-term production.

Trade barriers create new incentives for investment. Cars made in America were exempt from the import quota, which led Japanese automakers to invest in U.S.-based assembly facilities.

Production is a function of past policy and investment choices. Once assembly moved onshore, Japanese firms had incentives to onshore the rest of their value chain—production, research, and design—and they've chosen to continue their American investments long after the import quota was lifted.

Key Facts

Within a decade, the import quota generated:

$25+ billion in foreign capital investment (2022 dollars)

8 new auto assembly plants

300+ new production facilities

100,000+ new American jobs

Today, Honda and Toyota have among the highest domestic content of cars sold in America.

My father, like millions of other Americans, experienced both sides of the trade controversy. He traded in his expensive top-of-the-line Pontiac Catalina --- that stayed in the repair shop all the time because the oversized engine, air conditioner, automatic transmission, and electric windows constantly failed --- for a simple 4-cylinder Japanese-made Datsun with manual transmission and no air conditioner.

He also sold paint to a factory constructed in Macon, Georgia by YKK America, one of the first Japanese companies to relocate production to the USA. They brought many jobs to an economically depressed area. He said he liked doing business with the Japanese because he said they were loyal customers if you delivered the product when they requested and it worked according to spec. I hadn't thought of YKK in more than 40 years, but just looked up their Macon factory, and noticed they had just open a new one, augmenting several others they had built in Georgia during those decades:

YKK AP AMERICA INC. Operations Begin at New Macon Factory

High-Efficiency, Integrated Production Facility/Factory for Residential Vinyl Windows Established

Reagan's tariffs were effective in inducing many foreign companies to locate production to the United States, hiring our workers, and putting competitive pressure on our companies to improve quality and control costs. YKK has been in Georgia 45 years and kept expanding their operations to this day, a good deal for them and the Americans they employ and the American contractors like my Dad who supply them. And for American consumers who buy their products.

Opponents of tariffs say they protect inefficient industries with high costs of production that cause high prices to consumers, but the ones Reagan imposed increased competition and improved efficiency among our moribund motor vehicle industry, while lowering prices for consumers. Reagan's tariffs were removed as our industries got back on their feet. The Japanese, Korean, and German companies they induced to locate here are still adding value to our economy and providing good jobs for our people in the areas we most needed them. Nippon Steel has recently made an offer to buy U.S. Steel for $14 billion and invest in rebuilding its aging plant, perhaps because Trump's tariffs have made it more costly to import steel made in Japan.

Who Pays Tariffs?

"Tariffs are taxes on consumers," is a common objection to tariffs. Although it seems logical that the costs of tariffs would be passed to consumers, that cannot be known with certainty because, unlike a VAT, a tariff is only applied to one point in the supply chain --- the point of importation --- and therefore can be backloaded onto lower levels of the supply chain (by reducing profit margins of foreign suppliers and the importer) as well as passed up the supply chain the way a VAT is.

As *The Wall Street Journal* reported during Trump's first term, tariffs may be absorbed the foreign manufacturer and the American importer, without raising prices to consumers:

https://www.wsj.com/articles/u-s-apparel-industry-works-to-blunt-impact-of-tariffs-11566293401?mod=hp_lista_pos5

Apparel Companies Fear Tariffs Could Squash Profits

By Esther Fung and Inti Pacheco Updated Aug. 22, 2019, 11:52

About 40% of all clothing and 70% of shoes sold in U.S. are made in China

Macy's says it will work with its Chinese partners to absorb the extra costs associated with the tariffs.

Most apparel companies are expected to absorb the cost increase themselves or negotiate ways to cut expenses with their Chinese manufacturers to avoid antagonizing customers with higher prices.

"We learned from that experience that the customer had very little appetite for those cost increases," CEO Jeffrey Gennette said during the company's earnings call last week. Instead, he said, Macy's would work with its Chinese partners to absorb the extra costs.

General Motors also seemed able to absorb the tariffs by reducing its inflated profit margins producing in Mexico and selling in the U.S.:

GM CEO Mary Barra: Tariffs will cost us $5 billion, and prices 'will stay at the same level'

The Trump administration's tariffs on imported cars and auto parts will cost General Motors between $4 billion and $5 billion this year. But in an interview on CNN, CEO Mary Barra said the company doesn't necessarily expect to pass those higher costs onto consumers in the form of elevated prices.

"We believe ...pricing is going to stay at about the same level as it is," she told CNN's Erin Burnett Thursday,

Tariffs are more likely to be paid by consumers when the trade is between two developed countries with relatively high wages and costs of materials that produce relatively low profit margins for the companies producing and importing the product, because the profit margins are not high enough to absorb the tariff. If the product is made in a low-wage country, the profit margin is higher, enabling the tariff to be absorbed by the foreign producer and domestic importer. Such would be the case with tariffs on China and Mexico. But consumers should expect to pay the cost of tariffs on products from Canada, Japan, and the European Union, until companies in those countries relocate production to the United States or domestic competition enters the market, spawning a price war.

James Blaine felt that tariffs might in some circumstances lower consumer costs by increasing competition within the United States, by enticing new American companies to enter the business as well as foreign companies investing in production here:

The American protectionist...starts with the proposition that whatever is manufactured at home gives work and wages to our own people, and that even if the tariff is put so high as to prohibit the import of the foreign article, the competition of home producers will, according to the doctrine of Mr. Hamilton, rapidly reduce the price to the consumer.

.... This has notably been the result with respect to steel rails, the production of which in America has reached a magnitude surpassing that of England. Meanwhile rails have largely fallen in price to the consumer, the home manufacture has disbursed countless millions of [dollars of wages] among American laborers and has added largely to our industrial independence and to the wealth of the country.

Blaine, James Gillespie. Twenty Years of Congress, Vol. 1 From Lincoln to Garfield, with a Review of the Events Which Led to the Political Revolution of 1860. Kindle Edition.

An article in **Industry Week** stated that Trump's 25% tariffs on washing machines in 2018 through 2024 increased production in the United States while having no long-term effect on increasing prices:

Industry Week – OPINION:

The tariffs brought jobs and economic prosperity to two regions where appliances were not previously manufactured: Clarksville, Tennessee and Newberry, South Carolina.

Tariff opponents continue to repeat the falsehood that the tariffs raised washing machine prices. But washing machines fit a pattern we've seen with many of the 2018-2019 tariffs: After a brief price surge, consumer prices of the tariffed products fall, and tariffs have no noticeable effect on those prices afterwards.

Bearing in mind that **Industry Week** is a manufacturers' journal inclined to favor tariffs.

Tariffs and Jobs

There is no question that tariffs create or preserve *some* jobs. We see this every time we drive by the factories of Toyota, Honda, Nissan, Subaru, Mazda, Mitsubishi Kawasaki (engines), Volkswagen, BMW, Mercedes, Hyundai, KIA, YKK America, or Airbus Industries that located production here when Reagan imposed tariffs in the 1980s, or because Trump imposed them now. Also, jobs restored in America's homegrown companies:

https://youtu.be/Syzo-6dMoso?t=2659

Granite City, Illinois United States Steel Mill

"I was impacted two years ago when the plant was idled. Prior to that I worked here sixteen years and was able to provide a comfortable life for me and my family. Granted City works is home for me. Driving by the closed plant was difficult. Many families including my own suffered. It is great to see the plant up and running and everyone back to work and the community thriving.

Two years ago, like a lot of people in this room, I got a phone call that was a gut-wrenching call. I did not know how to pay the mortgage or keep my three boys in college. Thanks to Mr. Trump and everyone who supported him, we are back here now, things are better, and the future is looking bright.

Steel Mill, Latrobe, Pennsylvania

The president has saved the steel industry. You saved it with tariffs. You're my hero and the greatest president ever. We want to endorse you and give you a hard hat.

https://www.southstrandnews.com/news/a-new-era-celebration-marks-reopening-of-georgetown-steel-mill/article_6db8bee2-7899-11e8-8e22-f3f80f448489.html

A new era: Celebration marks reopening of Georgetown steel mill

By David Purtell Jun 25, 2018 "Reopening a closed down steel plant is a very special feeling," Gupta said. "When you see something coming back to life, it has a special place in itself."

https://www.nbc4i.com/news/politics/republic-steel-planning-to-reopen-ohio-plant-after-pres-trump-announced-tariffs/1096449097

Republic Steel planning to reopen Ohio plant after Pres. Trump announced tariffs

This could result in Republic bringing back 1,000+ jobs to its Lorain, OH facility.

https://www.constructiondive.com/news/texas-port-moves-16b-steel-factory-forward/522321

Texas port moves $1.6B steel factory forward

https://www.prnewswire.com/news-releases/nucor-to-build-rebar-micro-mill-in-florida-300612204.html

Nucor to Build Rebar Micro Mill in Florida

CHARLOTTE, N.C., March 12, 2018 /PRNewswire/ -- Nucor Corporation (NYSE: NUE) announced today that it will build a rebar micro mill in Frostproof, Florida, which is located in Polk County. This is a $240 million investment and is the second rebar micro mill Nucor is constructing. In November 2017, Nucor announced a rebar micro mill project in Sedalia, Missouri.

https://www.kbbonline.com/news/business/lg-electronics-breaks-ground-u-s-home-appliance-factory/

LG Electronics Breaks Ground on U.S. Home Appliance Factory

August 24, 2017

LG Electronics today broke ground on its new one-million-sq.-ft. home appliance manufacturing facility near Clarksville, Tenn. The project, in the heart of Montgomery County, is expected to bring at least 600 full-time jobs to the area and will accelerate the delivery of LG's innovative, premium home appliances to better meet U.S. consumer demand.

https://news.samsung.com/us/samsung-south-carolina-home-appliance-manufacturing-plant-investment-newberry/

Samsung to Expand U.S. Operations, Open $380 Million Home Appliance Manufacturing Plant in South Carolina

Samsung Newsroom 06.28.17

Newberry County facility will create 954 local jobs and support advanced R&D and production of premium home appliance products.

- *Import tariff brings 200 jobs to Clyde [Ohio] Whirlpool Jan. 23, 2018. More jobs are coming to the Clyde division of Whirlpool after President Donald Trump upheld a 50 percent tariff on imports of large residential washing machines.*

- *A new era: Celebration marks reopening of Georgetown steel mill By David Purtell Jun 25, 2018 "Reopening a closed down steel plant is a very special feeling," Gupta said. "When you see something coming back to life, it has a special place in itself."*

- *Republic Steel planning to reopen Ohio plant after Pres. Trump announced tariffs. This could result in Republic bringing back 1,000+ jobs to its Lorain, OH facility.*

- *Texas port moves $1.6B steel factory forward.*

- *Nucor to Build Rebar Micro Mill in Florida CHARLOTTE, N.C., March 12, 2018 /PRNewswire/ -- Nucor Corporation (NYSE: NUE) announced today that it will build a rebar micro mill in Frostproof, Florida, which is located in Polk County. This is a $240 million investment and is the second rebar micro mill Nucor is constructing. In November 2017, Nucor announced a rebar micro mill project in Sedalia, Missouri.*

- *LG Electronics (of South Korea) Breaks Ground on U.S. Home Appliance Factory August 24, 2017 LG Electronics today broke ground on its new one-million-sq.-ft. home appliance manufacturing facility near Clarksville, Tenn....expected to bring at least 600 full-time jobs to the area and will accelerate the delivery of LG's innovative, premium home appliances to better meet U.S. consumer demand.*

- *Samsung to Expand U.S. Operations, Open $380 Million Home Appliance Manufacturing Plant in South Carolina Samsung Newsroom 06.28.17 Newberry County facility will create 954 local* *jobs and support advanced R&D and production of premium home appliance products.*

- *Fiat Chrysler plans to open a new factory in Detroit, according to people briefed on the plan, the first new U.S. assembly plant to be opened by a major domestic car maker in at least a decade.*

The Whirlpool factory in Clyde, Ohio, on the verge of bankruptcy when Trump took office, now produces 22,000 washing machines a day and is hiring more workers, as **Industry Week** reported:

In January 2018, the Trump administration-imposed tariffs of 20% to 50% on large residential washing machines. The tariffs expired in February 2023. Six years after these tariffs were imposed, the U.S. now has a larger, more successful, and more competitive domestic washing machine industry.

The tariffs were a success, as measured by over 2,000 new jobs, more competition, no sustained effect on washing machine prices and economic stimulus with the construction of new factories.

The goal of industrial policies such as targeted tariffs should be to build domestic industries. Doing so creates growth, investment, employment and an upward trend in worker incomes. That has positive effects for the upstream and downstream industries that supply the appliance industry and the economy as a whole.

Six years later, we can see that the washing machine tariffs achieved precisely these goals.

The tariffs on washing machines induced South Korea's LG to relocate production to the U.S.:

https://softhandtech.com/are-lg-appliances-made-in-the-usa/

LG Appliances Made in the USA

Some of LG's manufacturing plants are located in the United States:

Hammond, Indiana: This plant focuses on producing washing machines and other laundry appliances. With the increasing demand for high-efficiency washers, this facility allows LG to cater to American consumers while boosting local job creation.

Clarksville, Tennessee: Opened in 2018, this facility showcases LG's commitment to local production. It primarily manufactures refrigerators, reflecting a strategy to minimize shipping times and costs while enhancing quality control.

These facilities not only provide jobs for thousands but also play a pivotal role in LG's supply chain, shortening delivery times and improving responsiveness to consumer trends.

The aluminum industry expanded capacity to keep pace with increased demand from manufacturing:

https://www.courier-journal.com/story/news/politics/2018/06/01/braidy-industries-breaks-ground-aluminum-mill-eastern-kentucky/646290002/

Braidy Industries breaks ground on Bevin-backed, $1.5B aluminum mill

Louisville Courier Journal Published June 1, 2018

Ashland, Kentucky, looks forward to Braidy Industries building an aluminum plant nearby that may boost the economy.

Braidy Industries broke ground Friday on a future, $1.5 billion aluminum rolling mill, sending a hopeful message to Eastern Kentuckians that it will help lead a long-awaited economic revival and keep its promise to create hundreds of high-paying jobs. "

139

It's an exciting moment for this area," said 68-year-old Tom Hilgendorf, of Ashland.

Business closures and mass layoffs have become commonplace in Eastern Kentucky, but Braidy expects its project to generate at least 1,000 construction jobs. The mill ... will employ about 600 people.

More jobs returned with Trump commenced his second term:

https://motorillustrated.com/stellantis-to-reopen-belvidere-plant-for-midsize-pickup-by-2027-battery-parts-projects-cancelled/151322/

Stellantis plans to restart operations at its shuttered Belvidere Assembly Plant in Illinois by early 2027 to produce a new Ram midsize pickup truck, local officials and union leaders confirmed. The trade-off is that the company has abandoned earlier plans to add a battery facility and large parts distribution hub at the site.

The timing of the announcement follows political pressure from President Donald Trump to increase domestic auto manufacturing and avoid tariffs on imports. Stellantis reversed previous plans to keep the site closed shortly after Trump assumed office in January. According to United Auto Workers officials, the decision was also influenced by union demands and strike threats.

"It'd be lying to say tariffs weren't a factor," said Kevin Gotinsky of the UAW Stellantis department, adding that internal union pressure was also critical. UAW President Shawn Fain and Stellantis North American manufacturing head Tim Fallon visited Belvidere earlier this month to review the company's timeline.

As well, South Korea's Hyundai announced major expansions of USA operations as a result o Trump's tariffs:

https://www.bbc.com/news/articles/cgkmvdz144vo

Hyundai unveils $21bn US expansion as Trump tariffs loom

25 March 2025

South Korean auto giant Hyundai has unveiled $21bn (£16.3bn) of investment in the US just days before President Donald Trump is set to impose new tariffs on trading partners.

The plan includes a new $5.8bn steel plant in the southern state of Louisiana.

Hyundai also said it will expand its American vehicle production and invest billions of dollars in new technology including autonomous driving and artificial intelligence (AI).

"This investment is a clear demonstration that tariffs very strongly work," Trump said during the event at the White House on Monday.

He added that more tariffs on vehicle imports are likely to be announced this week.

Hyundai said the new steelmaking facility will produce more than 2.7 million metric tons of steel a year and create more than 1,400 jobs.

It is expected to make steel for Hyundai's plants in Alabama and Georgia.

The announcement also included plans to invest $9bn to boost the firm's production in the US to 1.2 million vehicles a year by 2028.

Hyundai also said it had earmarked $6bn to expand partnerships with US firms to develop technologies including self-driving vehicles, robotics and AI.

On Wednesday, Hyundai Motor is set to hold an opening ceremony for a new $7.59bn car and battery factory in Georgia.

It already has a manufacturing facility in Alabama and its affiliate Kia has a factory in Georgia.

When fully operational, the three plants will have capacity to make a million vehicles a year, the company said.

Hyundai also said it would buy $3bn worth of liquefied natural gas (LNG) from the US.

Another auto company expanding operations in the U.S. is Audi:

https://www.cbtnews.com/audi-eyes-u-s-plant-to-counter-auto-tariffs/

Audi eyes U.S. plant to counter auto tariffs April 24, 2025

Audi is nearing a final decision on building its first U.S.-based factory, a critical stopgap that could help the automaker mitigate some of the impact of President Trump's 25% auto tariffs. During the auto show in Shanghai, Audi CEO Genot Döllner revealed that the company was moving toward a final decision and is currently considering several solutions.

Chinese-owned maker of refrigerators and stoves will add 1,000 jobs across five states

GE Appliances said it plans to invest $3 billion to expand and modernize its U.S. factories over the next five years, helping to blunt the effects of tariffs by reshoring some work now done in China and Mexico.

The investment will allow the factories to make new models of water heaters, air conditioners, gas ranges and refrigerators, and will create 1,000 jobs, the company said.

Kevin Nolan, GE Appliances' chief executive, said that while the company has long aimed to build its products close to their end markets, trade considerations played a role in the decision to upgrade its aging plants.

"I think it's become obvious with tariffs that building in the U.S. is a good thing right now," he said.

Once this round of investment has been completed, the company said it will have spent $6.5 billion on its U.S. factories and distribution network since 2016.

The friends of free trade resist this information about jobs returning to the United States by raising mutually exclusive objections:

"We can't re-shore manufacturing because

A) We don't have people who know how to work manufacturing [never mind that we fired the ones who knew it when we moved their work out of the country].

B) Our workers are paid too well; consumers can't afford to purchase products made in the USA.

C) "Reshoring manufacturing won't bring back any jobs because only robots and automation 'work' in manufacturing anymore."

D) When manufacturing is reshored, it's not because of tariffs. If the CEO says it is, it's only to placate Trump."

No matter how many jobs are re-shored after tariffs are enacted, the Free Trade Mavens will always claim it was for reasons having nothing to do with tariffs.

Tariffs and the National Debt

A timely report issued as this book is being revised for 2026 illustrates the effect of tariffs on diminishing the national debt:

https://www.thefinance360.com/tariff-revenue-surged-more-than-304-as-customs-duties-recorded-30-billion-after-us-deficit-decline/

Finance360 Jasmine Ara Sayyed February 12, 2026

Tariff Revenue Surged More Than 304%, As Customs Duties Recorded $30 Billion After US Deficit Decline

The U.S. government in January incurred a smaller deficit than it had a year earlier, though tariff collections were soaring, and a reminder of how crucial a long-awaited Supreme Court ruling might be to the fiscal health of the federal government.

Customs duties collected based on tariffs amounted to $30 billion for the month, bringing the fiscal year-to-date total to $124-billion, or 304 percent higher than the same period in 2025.

President Donald Trump initially imposed the duties in April 2025 at an across-the-board rate on all goods and services imported to the U.S., as well as a menu of so-called reciprocal tariffs on each country.

Since that time, the White House has been negotiating with its trading partners, withdrawing on some of the more aggressive charges while maintaining tough talk on issues.

However, the Supreme Court held oral arguments on the challenge to the auspices upon which Trump justified the tariffs last November. The decision was supposed to be in January.

The high court is yet to make its verdict, and there is worry in the white house that the failure to do so will push the U.S. into refunding the duties it has already collected. The tariffs assisted in obtaining a dent in the budget deficit rate.

The Treasury Department reported that the shortfall is estimated at approximately $95 billion in the fourth month of the fiscal year, a decline of about 26 percent compared to the same period a year ago.

That would make federal red ink $697 billion in the first quarter of the year, or 17 percent less than the same period of federal fiscal 2025, calendar-adjusted figures not being available. The deficit reduction is at 21 percent with calendar adjustments.

I do not dispute the conservative position that the federal budget deficit results from irresponsible spending by the federal government and has nothing directly to do with free trade vs. tariffs. For all we know, the irresponsible people in Congress will spend the $370 billion of tariff revenue, then increase spending by that much and more. But do we have any hope at all of closing the federal budget deficit without the $300 billion? We are in a state of demographic collapse whereby each generation only has half as many children as the prior generation. In two generations, 25% of the people will be paying 100% of the debt created by their grandparents.

Without taxing imports from other countries, the way we tax our own companies' profits, and the way other countries tax our exports with VATs, the ability of the United States government to remain a going concern may be nil. I know Libertarians will say that is a good thing, but it is more probable that we will elect politicians who will lower the boom on American taxpayers. Libertarians will respond that tariffs *are* taxes, so what's the difference, but I respond that some of the costs are absorbed by foreign suppliers, and that if the costs are not absorbed by foreigners, competition will spring up inside the United States to produce the product here, creating employment here, and supply chains here, all taxed.

Tariffs and National Security

Alexander Hamilton wrote in his Report on Manufactures:

Not only the wealth, but the independence and security of a country, appear to be materially connected with the prosperity of manufactures. Every nation, with a view to those great objects, ought to endeavor to possess within itself all the essentials of national supply.

I recalled this when I saw tonight's **Wall Street Journal** Editorial, advising us to offshore the construction of our navy to Japan and South Korea:

OPINION COMMENTARY [Follow]

Three Steps to Build America's Naval Power

Trump and the Pentagon should revamp procurement, let foreign yards maintain and build our warships, and increase the shipbuilding budget.

By Seth Cropsey
Feb. 12, 2025 5:43 pm ET

U.S. shipbuilding is constrained by an aging workforce and some yards that need technological investment. Absent a consistent budget, shipyards must rely on fluctuating congressional winds to ensure funding, making long-term plans impossible.

Greater shipyard capacity, however, requires long-term funding. The Ships Act, which would bolster U.S. commercial and naval shipbuilding, is a good start and has bipartisan support. But it doesn't move quickly enough. Pete Hegseth's Pentagon can take two immediate steps. First, it can contract with foreign yards, principally in Japan, South Korea and Europe, for routine maintenance and repair, easing the strain on U.S. yards and lowering costs. This will require political will, given opposition from maritime industry organized labor. Second, the Pentagon should push Congress to pass legislation to allow the purchase of warships from abroad. Korean yards in particular produce high-quality warships at competitive prices, while many allies can build essential combat support ships that the Navy currently lacks in sufficient numbers.

I commented:

In Michigan, I live across the lake from Manitowoc, Wisconsin, a town of about 30,000. The town's business used to be building lake freighters and pleasure boats. When WWII erupted, the U.S. Navy gave the shipbuilder a contract to build 32 submarines, one a month. The shipyard had never built subs before, but they got to work and built all 32 between 1942 and 1944. Floated them now the Illinois & Michigan canal to the Mississippi, then final assembly in New Orleans. And off they went to blockade Japan. 32 subs from one smallish town at a time when our population was 130 million. We had thousands of towns in those days that could do similar feats of prodigious production.

And now some are proposing to contract our Navy to Japan and South Korea because we no longer have shipyards If Trump's tariffs restore our industrial base to half of what it was, it might be just enough to prevent our defeat in the next war, if God forbid, there is one.

Tariffs to keep industry in the United States are a national security as well as economic matter. "We can convert a toaster factory in time of war into a drone factory, but we can't convert the rosewood offices of a multinational importing company into a drone factory." Were we to have a falling out with China, China's government might command the Japanese and South Koreans to stop supplying us with military and commercial products, and if they did not cease and desist, would destroy their ports to block the loading of their ships. Our navy, after depleting its missile inventory, would have to withdraw from the war. The ships we lost could not be replaced. It's the same with our missiles, tanks, and aircraft. What we built in hours in World War II now takes months and years. Our military cannot protect us if there is no civil manufacturing economy to back it up.

As the chart below shows, we are no longer the world's preeminent industrial economy. China's industrial GDP is twice as large as ours --- they manufacture 31.63% of the world's products, and we manufacture 15.87%:

https://worldpopulationreview.com/country-rankings/manufacturing-by-country

Share of World Manufacturing by Country

COUNTRY	MANUFACTURING ANNUAL VALUE (MIL) ◆	SHARE OF WORLD
China	$4,975,614	31.63%
United States	$2,497,132	15.87%
Japan	$1,025,092	6.52%
Germany	$751,339	4.78%
India	$450,862	2.87%
South Korea	$426,772	2.71%
Russia	$287,713	1.83%
South Korea	$426,772	2.71%
Russia	$287,713	1.83%

Tariffs vs. Subsidies

Our Congress has at long last awakened to the need to reshore critical industries like the production of computer chips. Alas, as is typical of Congress, it has done it in the worst possible way of offering government subsidies to chip-making companies that locate production to the United States.

The CHIPS and Science ACT was signed into law by President Biden authorizing $280 billion of federal subsidies of semiconductor chips manufactured in the United States. This is the worst possible way to promote the industry, because the subsidy is allocated to politically connected companies that donate to politicians, thereby advantaging them over smaller startup companies with better products that can't afford to lobby (bribe) politicians. The government has attached the usual strings of mandating the hiring people based on race and gender identity, rather than skills and competence. Much of the money will be wasted on companies run by cronies and families of politicians.

Wouldn't tariffs be the better way of brining the chips to the United States? A tariff of 25% on foreign chips would incentivize companies to relocate production here, without wasting government (taxpayer) money on political shenanigans. It would add money to our debt-ridden Treasury instead of depleting it. Established companies and upstarts would compete on the same terms, and the government would not have its nose in every company's business.

Tariffs and Luddites

THE LEADER of the LUDDITES

Free Traders like to associate tariffs with ancient things like buggy whips and old fuddy-duddies with names alike "Smoot" and "Hawley." Skeptics of free trade are likened to the fictional "Ned Ludd," an imaginary character who supposedly roamed the British countryside in the wee hours of moonlit nights the early 1800's, wrecking factories in hopes of protecting the labor of home-spinners and blacksmiths operating out of cottages and barns. According to Free Trade Maven lore, the Luddites have nowadays switched roles, from wanting to destroy factories to save obsolete cottage industries in the 1700s, to wanting to destroy the high-tech economy with tariffs to save obsolete factories in the 2000s. The friends of free trade want to hustle American jobs off to cheap labor countries so American companies don't have to spend money investing in robots and automation in the United States.

Another favorite canard of free traders is "buggy whips" --- the sticks with leather thongs used to beat slow horses pulling old wagons before Henry Ford put the wagons and the horses out to pasture. The implication is that the friends of tariffs want to protect obsolete jobs that have no place in the modern world. "You want to protect the buggy whip industry with tariffs! Ha! Ha! at you!"

This is a false analogy, because we never put our buggy whip makers out of work by shipping their jobs to Mexico and China. They transitioned to making automobiles as the motor vehicle industry developed in the United States. When Henry Ford started building his cars at the end of the 19th Century, his workers were experienced in building steam engines, running electrical wiring, and transmitting energy to the wheels of trains and horse-drawn wagons. If we'd offshored all those pre-existing jobs to other countries, we could not have established the motor vehicle industry here.

Free Traders are prone to claiming that industry today occupies the same position in our economy as agriculture did in the early 1800s when about half of Americans earned their livelihoods from farming. That proportion shrunk steadily to about 1% of Americans today. The free traders say, "That's progress, when 1% of the people can feed themselves and the other 99%. It's like that with industry. All those people put out of work will move on to higher value jobs." However:

1) We did not offshore our agriculture to other countries. In fact, we protect it ferociously with government subsidies, plus importing millions of cheap-labor foreigners to work the fields. In that regard, no improvements in labor productivity have been made in 10,000 years.

2) The people most vociferously against protecting high-paying manufacturing jobs say we should load the country with indigent laborers earning minimum wage at best, stooping low in the fields, picking, with their bare hands, acres up acres of berries, lettuce, cabbages, and turnips instead of automating the process with machinery.

3) They do not understand the automation of industry creates a structure of automation support. If the industry goes overseas, the automation industry goes with it

4) **They will not understand that industrial jobs are necessary even when operations are automated, and that the higher-level jobs in tuning the robots, planning the production,**

supervising the quality control, are unlikely to be replaced by automation, and if they are, the automation can be done here. .

5) Free Traders protect agriculture because they haven't figured out how to relocate farms out of the country. If they could devise a transporter beam to transmit American dirt to cheap labor countries Mexico and China, they would do it, in the same way they have exported American factories to those countries.

6) Free traders want us to believe that American jobs go to Mexico and China "because that's where the robots are" but when you look at what's next to the factories, it is shacktowns of human being workers if it is in Mexico and enormous dormitories of people who can't afford to live anywhere else if it is China.

When opponents of tariffs are forced to confront these headlines of jobs saved and created by tariffs, their fallback is to claim that the jobs were created at exorbitant cost to consumers, and thereby ultimately caused more jobs to be lost. They cannot prove jobs are lost to tariffs, so they resort to torturing the data until it screams "tariffs cost jobs...now take off the thumbscrews.

Tariffs as Tortured Data

Free traders are not above inventing false data to boost their positions when the facts are against them. This happened with the steel tariff imposed by President George W. Bush in 2002, when free traders invented false data purporting to show employment in steel industries fell, when in truth it rose. This hoax was resurrected during Trump's first steel tariffs of 2018, and I expect will be resurrected now that he has announced steel tariffs for his second term. Here is the hoax document purporting price increases and job losses for the 2002 steel tariffs:

TRADE PARTNERSHIP WORLDWIDE, LLC

The Unintended Consequences of U.S. Steel Import Tariffs:
A Quantification of the Impact During 2002

Executive Summary

As a result of a Section 201 ("safeguard") investigation brought at the behest of the U.S. steel industry, President Bush in March 2002 imposed tariffs on imports of certain steel products for three years and one day. The tariffs, combined with other challenges present in the marketplace at the time and in the months that followed, boosted steel costs to the detriment of American companies that use steel to produce goods in the United States. The resulting negative impact included job losses for thousands of American workers.

The Consuming Industries Trade Action Coalition (CITAC) Foundation requested a formal examination of the impact of higher steel costs on American steel-consuming industries,1and in particular, a quantification of employment losses at those companies. This study employed straight-forward and widely accepted regression analysis using a variety of price and employment data to maximize the reliability of the results.

We found that:

157

• *200,000 Americans lost their jobs to higher steel prices during 2002. These lost jobs represent approximately $4 billion in lost wages from February to November 2002.*

• *Job losses escalated steadily over 2002, peaking in November (at 202,000 jobs), and slightly declining to 197,000 jobs in December.4*

• *More American workers lost their jobs in 2002 to higher steel prices than the total number employed by the U.S. steel industry itself (187,500 Americans were employed by U.S. steel producers in December 2002).*

Charts 1 and 2 show actual employment relative to what employment would have been in the absence of increases in steel prices on a monthly basis.

However, their data reports precisely the opposite, that employment in steel-consuming industries increased by 300,000 *after* Bush imposed tariffs:

Chart 1

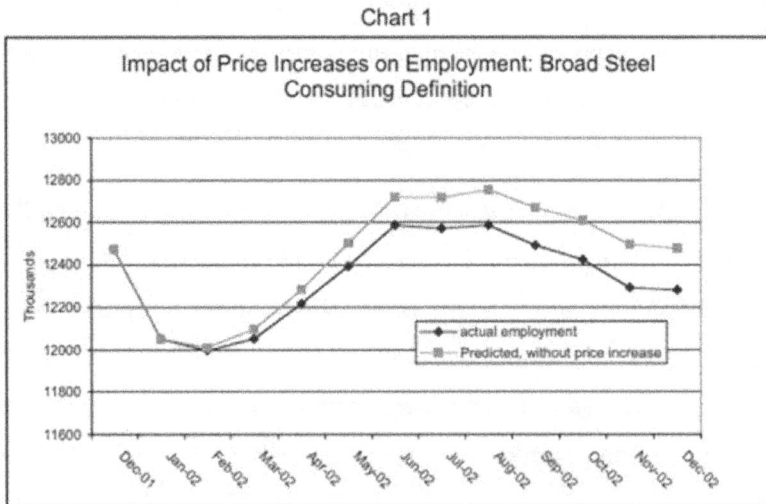

Impact of Price Increases on Employment: Broad Steel Consuming Definition

The chart begins with a fraudulent datapoint:

On March 5, 2002, President Bush imposed tariffs on imports of many steel products into the United States for three years and one day. The duties became effective March 20, 2002.

If we take December 2001 as a "benchmark" for steel prices, *then higher steel costs reduced steel-consuming sector employment in December 2002 by roughly 200,000 (of that, 50,000 jobs were lost to higher steel costs in the metal manufacturing, machinery and equipment and transportation equipment and parts sectors). Steel-consumers have lost more jobs to higher steel costs than the total number employed by steel producers in December 2002 (187,500). These lost jobs represent about $4 billion in lost wages from February / November 2002, assuming workers found new jobs within four weeks.*

The tariffs were announced on March 5, 2002 and became effective on March 20, 2002. So why backdate the starting point to December 2001? When steel tariffs were announced, employment in the steel consuming industries was about 12,000,000 (lower blue line). When the study ended in December 2002, it was about 12,300,000. Those are real numbers showing that employment increased fastest when the tariff was enacted. The green line above the blue line purports to show that employment would have theoretically been higher, but it is a fraudulent number invented by the authors through "regression analysis," meaning they pulled it out of their backsides, as they were paid by the steel consuming consortium who opposed the tariffs The authors even admitted they had little confidence in their conclusion:

*How many of these job losses [there were no real job losses, only job gains] are attributable to high steel prices [supposedly due to tariffs]? **This is not an easy question to answer.***

Another fiction is their claim that jobs were lost because tariffs caused steel prices to rise. But steel prices were at the low end of their decades-long trading range in 2002 and did not start rising rapidly until the tariffs were rescinded at the end of 2003:

https://pubs.usgs.gov/sir/2012/5188/sir2012-5188.pdf

Table 1.   Annual average hot-rolled steel bar price.

[Values in dollars per one hundred pounds]

Year	Price
1984	22.08
1985	24.10
1986	24.10
1987	17.12
1988	17.25
1989	19.60
1990	20.43
1991	20.60
1992	17.48
1993	18.44
1994	18.95
1995	18.95
1996	18.95
1997	19.75
1998	18.75
1999	17.47
2000	17.00
2001	17.00
2002	17.66
2003	18.58
2004	27.32
2005	35.96
2006	41.90
2007	36.09
2008	50.41
2009	35.64
2010	42.17

Steel prices soared *after the tariffs were removed* because the economy came out of recession in 2002 (following the 9/11 terrorist

160

attacks) and went into an inflationary boom as the economy got back on its feet:

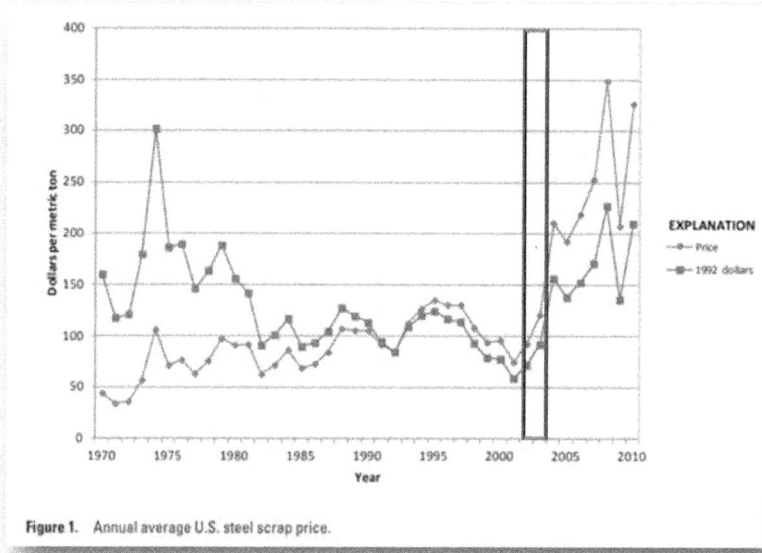

Figure 1. Annual average U.S. steel scrap price.

The only effect of the tariffs was to encourage the purchase of made-in-USA steel, instead of buying surplus steel dumped in the United States by government-subsidized mills in China and the European Union.

Next come the recurring microcosms of anti-tariff propaganda, claiming tariffs cause more jobs to be lost than are saved, when the facts prove the opposite. A typical misdirection from *The Wall Street Journal* was a story first reported in 2018 with the first round of Trump's tariffs, and resurrected in February 2025 as propaganda against his current round of tariffs on steel and aluminum:

https://www.wsj.com/opinion/donald-trump-25-percent-tariffs-steel-aluminum-manufacturing-business-28c1f839?mod=opinion_lead_pos3

The Truth About Trump's Steel Tariffs

His first-term levies hurt consumers and U.S. manufacturers.

Consider Mid-Continent Steel and Wire, which produced roughly half of the nails made in the U.S. After the steel tariffs [of 2018] took effect, its sales plunged by more than half, causing it to lay off 80 workers. Another 120 quit because they worried its Missouri factory might close. After this damage, the Commerce Department granted the company a tariff exemption.

The truth is that the company laid off the workers because housing was in recession in 2018 due to the Federal Reserve making four interest rate increases, spooking the housing markets, as Bloomberg reported:

The U.S. Housing Market Looks Headed for Its Worst Slowdown in Years

Updated on July 26, 2018, 12:41

The U.S. housing market -- particularly in cutthroat areas like Seattle, Silicon Valley and Austin, Texas -- appears to be headed for the broadest slowdown in years.

The orders fell, because when houses are in "the worst slowdown in years" builders are not buying nails. Nor did they disclose that Mid-Continent steel is owned by a Mexican steel company. The company could just as well have bought its steel from a U.S. supplier to avoid the tariff, assuming there was any demand for nails, which there wasn't.

Another howler of anti-tariff propaganda was twisted out of the beer industry:

https://www.wsj.com/articles/how-tariffs-lead-to-more-tariffs-11574636899

How Tariffs Lead to More Tariffs

Steel makers asked for protection. A keg maker did next. Now brewers?

Nov. 24, 2019 6:08 pm ET

There's a nursery rhyme about an old lady who swallowed a fly—then swallowed a spider to catch the fly, then swallowed a bird to catch the spider, and on it goes, all the way up to a horse. Protectionist trade policies can be like that.

At the behest of steel makers who griped about foreign competition, President Trump last year imposed a 25% tariff on imported steel. At that time, we reported on the collateral damage to American Keg Co., which says it's the only U.S. maker of stainless-steel beer kegs. With metal prices rising, American Keg divulged it had laid off a third [10] of its 30 workers. "We're very concerned," the CEO said, "that this could put us out of business."

Direct and indirect jobs in the beer business are down 40,000 since 2016, trade groups said this spring. The Beer Institute's CEO has called Mr. Trump's aluminum tariffs "an anchor on a vibrant industry." The logical conclusion is to fizz up breweries by levying tariffs on foreign beer: Corona, Heineken, Sapporo, you name it. Our teetotalling President won't mind.

This is how Donald's Trump protectionism, like Barack Obama's overregulation, gradually leaches economic growth with compounding political intervention.

First, note that 10 (ten) people supposedly lost their jobs making stainless steel beer kegs because of Trump's tariffs on steel. Compare that anti-tariff propaganda to what the "beer study' cited in the article actually says:

The [beer] industry report noted that while overall beer sales are down about 2.4 percent from 2016, there are some areas of growth, with brewing jobs up 8 percent. It attributed the increase to "tremendous growth in micro and brewpub employment as well as growth in higher margin products from all brewers."

The number of distributor jobs alone in the industry has also increased by more than 19 percent over the past decade,

The total number of brewing facilities has grown by 1,191 in two years – most being very small brewers or brewpubs.

There continues to be a shift away from less expensive products to more expensive local and "craft" beers....

Consumers purchase smaller volumes of these higher priced beers than they do of less expensive domestic light lagers and pilsners, suggesting that fewer employees are required to serve beer in a given bar or tavern.

The steel keg people lost their jobs because beer sales declined 2.4%, the decline concentrated in cheap beers sold in kegs. People were buying higher quality beer in glass bottles, instead of swilling cheap brews. The layoffs of 10 people in the beer keg company have nothing at all to do with tariffs. The business press, which never cared about 10 *million* laid off when their jobs were moved to Mexico and China, is trying to make out like the layoffs of 10 people at the aluminum keg company will sink our entire economy.

The current complaint is that the price of eggs is high because people are bidding up the price now to get ahead of Trump's proposed new tariffs. The truth is that the price of eggs went up 15% in a year because a bird flu epidemic killed the chickens.

Non-Tariff Trade Barriers

After Trump imposed broad tariffs, many non-reciprocating trading partners proposed trade deals of "zero tariffs." Some pleas for zero tariffs came from countries like Israel, who we have free trade agreements with us and should already be trading with reciprocally with zero tariffs. The other countries are all members of GATT / WTO who should be trading reciprocally with tariffs not exceeding 2.5% on manufactured goods and 5% on farm products. So, why are they inflicting huge trade deficits on us, such as the $235 billion from the European Union, a supranational entity supposedly purposed for free trade?

The answer is that non-reciprocating trade countries are cartels of manufacturers, distributors, retailers, banks, and government agencies with interlocking boards of directors that only buy from within their own countries whenever they can, not from external markets like the United States. The European Union is a closed market cartel of multiple countries that only buys product from the United States that doesn't compete with domestic products. Every Asian country, especially China, operates on these terms. The promise of "zero tariffs" is merely a plan to induce the United States to remove the tariffs Trump imposed, while they continue the informal barriers of not buying from the United States. Recall that China promised in 2003 to "buy millions of tons of U.S. beef" and never bought an ounce for 14 years.

In the first weeks of his second term, President Trump used the threat of tariffs to leverage Canada and Mexico into improving their border control, to stop the United States from inundation by people with no legal right to be here. He has imposed an additional 10% tariff on top of those in his first term (maintained by President Biden) to induce

China's government to reduce the manufacture of the deadly drug fentanyl Chinse companies illegally export to the United States.

What leverage, other than tariffs do we have? Most other countries have less robust legal systems than ours. Will any Chinese company be successfully sued in China for infringing on the patents of an American company? Even if some international body like the World Trade Organization rules against China, there's no enforcement mechanism to compel Chinese companies to abide by the decision. The WTO exists only to harass countries like the United States, who have large markets the other countries depend on for their prosperity, not to give us relief from trade predators.

Our tariff skeptics say, "Don't put tariffs on those countries. All we need to do is tell them to stop stealing our IP [intellectual property] and sue them if they don't." But since no American company receives a fair hearing in a Chinese court, there is no enforcement mechanism to assure fair trade with our products, other than our imposing tariffs on theirs

"But wouldn't American consumers pay the cost of the tariffs?" respond the Free Traders. "Why should we make Americans pay for Chinese crimes?" For the same reason that we don't let Americans legally purchase merchandise stolen from other Americans. If China is harming our companies and their employees with unfair trade practices --- and some aggressively illegal ones like stealing IP with cyber attacks ---why should we buy anything from China? Isn't that like buying stolen property for a thief who burglarized your neighbor's house?

I don't believe Free Traders care about China's IP theft. "Yes, we need to stop China stealing our IP, but tariffs are not the way to go about it," is their response. All they care about is buying cheap Chinese imports.

Alternatives to Tariffs

It may be useful to place tariffs in context with other taxes on trade. The closest next-of-kin of the tariff is the VAT, the VAT taxing domestic and foreign products at all points along the supply chain from manufacture to retail sail, whereas tariffs tax only imported items, and only once, at the port of entry.

After World War II, the nations of Western Europe began considering economic integration to prevent future antagonisms from inflaming wars. They wanted free trade between their countries but knew that businesses would gravitate toward producing in smaller tax-haven countries while extracting the lion's share of their profits by selling into the larger and higher taxed countries. If they wanted to integrate their economies, they needed to devise a system of dual taxation that enabled countries to levy corporate income taxes on companies with headquarters and production facilities inside their borders but also levied taxes at the intermediate points adding value, including at the point of sale.

In the 1950s, European countries developed the dual taxation system of the corporate income tax plus value added (VAT) taxes at points of intermediate processing and sale. Assume a company headquartered in Germany sells it to a distributor in Belgium for $100, who sells it to a retailer in France for $150, who sells it to a consumer for $200. Assuming the VAT in each country is 20%, the VAT taxation chain is:

1) The suppliers that provided the inputs to the German manufacturer (there could be many companies in the supply chain) cumulatively paid VATs of 20% * $60 = $12 to Germany's government.

2) The German company adds a VAT of $20 to the $100 it charges the Belgian distributor. But since its supply chain has already paid $12, it owes the German government $20 - $12 = $8.

3) The Belgian distributor adds its 20% VAT of $30 to the $150 it charges to the French retailer. But since it has already paid a $20 VAT it paid on $100, it owes the Belgian government $10.

4) The French retailer adds a 20% VAT to the $200 it charges the consumer, making the final selling price to the consumer $240, $200 + the $20% VAT of $40. But since the French company already paid $30 for the VAT the Belgian company paid, it owes the French Government $10.

5) The cumulative vat is $12 supply chain plus $8 manufacturer for Germany's government, $10 for Belgium's government, and $10 for France's government, adding up to $40 dollars on $240 of final value at point of sale.

6) Every party in the transaction chain also pays a corporate income tax to its government on the year's accumulated profits. VAT is the heavier tax, because it cannot be fudged with deprecation, write-offs, and other intangible costs the way corporate income tax is. It pushes up to the consumer, ultimately equaling the VAT percentage of the final sales price, whereas the corporate income tax looks downward on the accumulation of costs of goods sold, overhead, deductions, and so on, such that companies may use "creative accounting" to negate some or all of it. The two taxes together raise prices to the consumer more than either would alone, the VAT being the more costly to the consumer. It is also complicated to administer, because a product may have

dozens of cost inputs, each with a VAT, that gets deducted from the VAT each company owes to its government. Accounting departments, and the overhead expense they cost companies, are onerous in countries with VATs.

If the product is imported from the United States into Europe, the first VAT applied in 2), since the United States does not impose a VAT on the value of production in the United States.

Now let's consider the scenario where the product is made in Germany and brought into the United States by a distributor who pays $100, who sells it to an American retailer for $150, who sells it to an American customer for $200.

1) The Germany company and its supply chain don't pay a VAT since the product is sent to the United States, a country outside the European Union trade zone.

2) The $100 of value created in Germany is not taxed by the United States, since we do not have a VAT. The American importer pays a corporation income tax on the $50 of profit it earns when it sells to an American retailer for $150.

3) The American retailer pays a corporation income tax on the $50 of profit when sells to an American consumer for $200, and with most products it must charge the American consumer a sales tax. Sales tax is not paid if the item is sold to a company that uses it as an input to manufacture some other product.

The $100 of value produced in Germany is only taxed at the retail sales level in the US, and not even then if it is imbedded in another company's cost of production and not sold to the public as a finished product. This lowers the cost to American consumers, because the importer doesn't have to collect the VAT at the port of entry the way importers in VAT-charging companies do. Americans are generally wealthier than Europeans of comparable income, because we don't pay a VAT on domestic or foreign products. But imports are taxed less by the United States than domestic products that incur corporation income taxes and employee / employer payroll taxes on all the work done in the United States. That is why imports are deducted from the GDP, because the work of producing them is done outside the United States. Imposing a VAT would be the noncontroversial way for the United States to gin tax revenues on foreign production but would have to be applied equally to domestic production, thereby creating all the price inflation and bureaucracy burdens of VATs.

European countries developed the VAT system because they are small countries grouped closely together, so it is easy for a company to locate their operations in tax-haven countries like Switzerland, Luxembourg, and Ireland, while milking tax free profits out of the large market countries of France and Germany. The VAT assures taxing wherever value is added, either by production or distribution markups.

VATs were never considered in the United States because we are a continental market unified under a true national government, where companies have only recently begun to use tax shelter countries to extract profits tax-free from the United States. Nor do Americans desire a VAT tax, because the last thing companies want is another alternative tax system layered on top of the corporation tax system. Nor is there any doubt that VATs raise prices to consumers, because they roll up into a 20% or higher national sales tax. On the plus side, VATs don't create trade controversies when both trading partners have them, because both countries tax each other's exports the same way.

However, the VAT tax becomes asymmetrical when one trading partner has it and another doesn't. Most countries impose a VAT on imports from the U.S., the same as they tax their domestic production. We don't have a VAT to tax other countries exports to the United States. The other countries say: "If you want to tax our exports to the U.S., then you should apply a VAT that taxes your domestic productions, so it doesn't discriminate against our exports." The United States is equally entitled to say. "If you tax our exports with a VAT, we are entitled to tax your exports to us with a tariff. If you don't think that's fair, then abolish *your* VAT."

In 2018, former Republican House Ways and Means Committee Chairman Kevin Brady proposed a hybrid tax he calls the Border Adjustment VAT (BAVAT). Because VAT taxes are levied by every significant country except the United States, Kevin Brady's felt the BAVAT would be less controversial than a plain vanilla tariff.

Brady proposed a BAVAT of 20% * (USA revenues – USA cost inputs). Companies that produce in the USA would deduct all those costs before calculating the 20% BAVAT. An imported item having no USA cost inputs would be taxed at the full 20%.

The Border Adjustment VAT would be applied according to these circumstances:

#1 A product may be produced in the USA and sold in the USA.

#2 A product may be produced in another country and sold in the USA.

#3 A product may be produced in the USA and sold in another country.

#4 An American-owned company may establish a foreign subsidiary to produce products for sale in the foreign country's market.

The taxes on the four scenarios are:

#1 A product is produced in the USA with $8,000 of cost inputs and sold for $10,000 in the USA. The BAVAT tax is: ($10,000 - $8,000) * 20% = **$400**. We should allow the U.S. company to deduct its corporate income tax against the BAVAT, so the BAVAT could even be zero. This applies to subsidiaries of foreign companies that produce in the USA, so any company, domestic or foreign, that produces here gets the low end of the BAVAT.

#2 A product is imported into the USA and sold for $10,000. The tax is: ($10,000 - zero) * 20% = **$2,000**.

#3 Product is produced in the USA with $8,000 of cost inputs and exported to another country where it is sold for $10,000. This generates a **REBATE of $1,600** on (USA revenues of zero, minus $8,000 of USA cost inputs) = * 20%. A company that produces in the USA and earns most of its revenues abroad will receive a tax rebate from our government on its corporate income taxes.

#4 Product is produced overseas by an American company and sold overseas. No tax event because no USA revenues or cost inputs are incurred.

The BAVAT would tax product made in the USA lightly, while imports having no USA cost inputs are taxed at full 20%. Exports would receive a rebate because an American company is producing product in the USA and thereby paying wages to Americans and taxes to our governments. Countries that trade fairly and reciprocally could be assed BAVAT as if they were parts of the United States, deducting their cost inputs as our companies do.

However, the BAVAT has gained no traction in Congress or with the public because it is after all a hybrid tax containing all the computation and administrative complications of computing a VAT based on sales price minus compounded supply chain costs, while still having a tariff character of taxing imports higher than domestic productions. The most advantageous part of it is that "Border Adjustment VAT" sounds more modern than "tariff."

Another tariff alternative is managed trade cartels assigning production quotas for each country in the cartel. Our first and only managed trade cartel was the *Auto Pact* signed by the United States and Canada n 1965. It established a tariff-free common market between the USA and Canada in motor vehicles and parts, with the stipulation that value added in each country would be proportional to motor vehicles sales in each country. For every $10 of motor vehicle value created in the U.S., $1 must be created in Canada. Customers in both countries could purchase vehicles made in either country tariff free. The agreement remained in force until superseded by NAFTA in 1994. If the USA/Canada Auto Pact were revived with Mexico as a partner, the USA would be allocated 85% of production for the three countries, Canada 11%, and Mexico 4% of cars sold in North America, instead of the current 68% USA, 9% Canada, and 23% Mexico. Auto companies operating in Mexico would be permitted to export no more than 360,000 motor vehicles into the United States instead of the current 3 million. That would be an alternative way of limiting Mexico's role as a labor substitution market primarily used to disemploy American auto workers.

Import quotas are another trade management strategy implemented by President Reagan to limit imports of motor vehicles and electronics from Japan as described in the *President Regan's Selective*

Tariffs section. They induced Japanese, German, and South Korean companies to produce in the USA. Tariffs are favored by President Trump's administration as being more flexible allowing foreign producers and consumers to decide whether to pay the tariff to buy products made in other countries, or to move the production inside the tariff wall around the United States.

Constitutionality of Presidential Tariffs

The constitutional question of whether Trump is authorized to levy tariffs without consent of Congress will soon be decided by the Supreme Court. Because countries are so hypocritical about practicing free trade, our Congress decided the president should be empowered to wield tariffs as a bargaining chip to induce recalcitrant countries to lower their trade barriers on American products, or in extreme circumstances to impose the tariffs for as long as necessary to protect American industries and their workers. As we've seen, the most prolific imposer of tariffs under this authority before Trump's second term was President Reagan, who, though a free trader at heart, saw his first duty as protecting the livelihoods of American workers and their industries from rapacious foreign competition that only wanted to sell in the United States without buying reciprocally.

Trump says he enacted the tariffs under the authority delegated to presidents by beginning with President John F. Kennedy, to levy tariffs during "trade "emergencies" the president believes inflicts significant harm on our economy. Presidents Nixon and Reagan imposed tariffs broadly, Nixon citing the collapse of the dollar following our repudiation of the gold standard in 1973, and Reagan imposing tariffs on manufactured products from many countries to buy time for our companies to retool for enhanced productivity. President Biden imposed a 100% tariff on Chinese electric vehicles that Trump continues, as well as letting the Commerce Department increase the tariff on certain categories of Canadian lumber. These tariffs fit the character of the delegation of tariff authority to the president by Congress.

Some of Trump's tariffs, like the ones on specific products of steel, aluminum, and motor vehicles, and also the general tariffs on blatantly unfair trade partners like China, are more in compliance with the intent of Congress, and in keeping with past presidential tariff precedents, than the whimsical ones he has enacted, such as a 50% tariff on Brazil because he alleged its government ran an unfair election, or the tariff he threatened to impose on the European Union if they didn't stop opposing his initiative to annex Greenland by coercion. Trump's revenue tariffs of 10% to 20% on most countries are based on the theory that the trade deficit of nearly $1 trillion a year is a self-evident emergency, an assertion that has no precedent. I am expecting the Supreme Court to uphold some tariffs based on Congressional intent and precedent, while setting expiration dates on the rest unless approved by Congress.

The Constitution empowers only Congress to levy tariffs. However, Congress has delegated some of its authority to presidents on six prior occasions:

https://constitutioncenter.org/blog/how-congress-delegates-its-tariff-powers-to-the-president

How Congress delegates its tariff powers to the president

April 2, 2025 | by Scott Bomboy

Laws That Allow the President to Impose Tariffs

According to the Congressional Research Service, there are six statutory provisions currently in place that control how the president and the executive branch can use tariffs. Three provisions require federal agency investigations before a tariff can be imposed. The other provisions do not require an investigation before actions are taken.

Section 232 of the Trade Expansion Act of 1962 has been used by the first and second Trump administrations for steel and aluminum

178

imports. It authorizes the president to ask the Secretary of Commerce to determine if goods are being imported in manner that threatens national security. The secretary then reports back to the president if he has any affirmative findings. "Section 232 does not require the President to follow the Secretary's recommendations but permits him to take alternative actions or no action," the CRS says. Under Section 232, there is no maximum time limit on the president's tariff actions.

Another provision that requires an investigation is Section 201 of the Trade Act of 1974. The act allows the president to impose tariffs if the U.S. International Trade Commission (ITC) finds that an import surge is threatening a U.S. domestic industry. If the ITC makes an affirmative determination, the president can take action accordingly, including placing tariffs. Tariffs imposed under Section 201 are not meant to be permanent, and the actions have a limit of four to eight years.

Section 301 of the Trade Act of 1974 allows the United States Trade Representative (USTR) to authorize tariffs on foreign countries that restrict U.S. commerce in "unjustifiable," "unreasonable," or "discriminatory" ways. If the USTR confirms such behavior after an investigation, the president has the discretion to allow the USTR to impose tariffs for at least four years.

Among the three provisions that allow the president to act on his own to impose tariffs without an investigation, only one has ever been used: the International Emergency Economic Powers Act of 1977. The act allows the president to declare an emergency under the National Emergency Act (NEA) and then use his extensive economic powers to regulate or prohibit imports. The CRS says that President Trump was the first chief executive to use this act in February 2025, when he announced tariffs on Canada, China, and Mexico. The emergency stated by the president can be terminated at this request, or by a joint resolution of Congress.

Section 122 of the Trade Act of 1974, which allows the president to enact temporary tariffs to address "large and serious United States balance-of-payments deficits" or certain other situations that present "fundamental international payments problems; and Section 338 of Tariff Act of 1930, which authorizes the president to enact "tariffs on articles produced by, or imported on the vessels of, foreign countries that discriminate against U.S. commerce in certain ways," have not yet been used.

Ultimately, Congress can limit or expand the presidential tariffs powers through legislation, but the CRS concludes that based on precedents dating back to the time of Chief Justice Marshall, judicial precedent "has given the President broad latitude to exercise his tariff authorities."

Scott Bomboy is the editor in chief of the National Constitution Center.

The conservative-leaning **New York Sun** editorialized the delegation of Congress' Constitutional authority to levy tariffs as a one-way street that once handed off to the President, can not be reclaimed, unless the Supreme Court reclaims it for them:

NEW YORK

The Sun

EDITORIALS

Tariffs: The 'One-Way Ratchet'

A revolt brewing in Congress seeks to reclaim the legislature's authority, granted in the Constitution, to do the laying and collecting of tariffs.

THE NEW YORK SUN

Feb 11, 2026, 03:20 PM ET

Congress is moving closer to a rebuke of President Trump's tariff regime, but the incipient rebellion will likely prove futile. That underscores how hard it is for the legislators to reclaim powers that they have ceded to the commander-in-chief. The power to set tariffs was granted in the Constitution to Congress. Yet the legislators over the years delegated away much of their authority on this head. "A one-way ratchet," Justice Neil Gorsuch called it in November.

"We are going to do Canada today and follow with Mexico," says the ranking Democrat on the House Foreign Affairs Committee, Congressman Greg Meeks. Votes in the House against tariffs imposed on Brazil, and Mr. Trump's worldwide "Liberation Day" levies, are also on deck, Mr. Meeks told Axios. The votes of three House Republicans paved the way for anti-tariff measures, which for months the GOP leadership has staved off via procedural rules.

The Senate, for its part, has already approved four resolutions that oppose Mr. Trump's tariffs on, say, Canada, Brazil, and other nations across the globe. Yet even if the two houses of Congress can pass identical bills opposing the tariffs, it is doubtful that the measures would survive an anticipated presidential veto. Overturning a veto requires a two-thirds vote by each house. That suggests an element of political theater in these anti-tariff votes.

Justice Gorsuch queried Mr. Trump's solicitor general, John Sauer, on this head. Speaking to General Sauer, the justice said "you emphasize that Congress can always take back its powers." Yet, Justice Gorsuch asked, "don't we have a serious retrieval problem here?" After all, "once Congress delegates by a bare majority and the President signs it,"

Justice Gorsuch said, "Congress can't take that back without a super majority."

As a result, the justice continued, that "Congress, as a practical matter, can't get this power back once it's handed it over to the President." He described this process as "a one-way ratchet" toward the "gradual but continual accretion of power in the executive branch and away from the people's elected representatives." Justice Gorsuch mused: "What president's ever going to give that power back?"

During the great national emergency of the Civil War, President Lincoln took many emergency measures that were not explicitly authorized by the Constitution as presidential powers. He said that before enacting any of these novel measures, he asked, "Is it Constitutional [within the intent of the Founders who wrote the Constitution] and if it is Constitutional, is it expedient."

The Supreme Court must decide on the Constitutionality of Congress delegating its power to tax to the President, and if that is Constitutional, are Trump's tariffs expedient. Trump's tariffs have the character of being levied on his personal authority without the force of enduring law an Act of Congress has. Any future president can repeal them at will, if the Supreme Court does not do it first.

Closing Statements

Those who view tariffs primarily from the perspective of consumption --- of being able to purchase products at the lowest cost when other countries supply them for less --- oppose tariffs. They believe consumption is preeminent over production because they say the only means of acquiring a surplus of capital is to consume less than we produce. If imports lower the cost of consumption over what we can purchase domestically, we should buy them, because that frees our dollars to invest in creating new enterprises that produce higher value goods and services that pay higher wages and earn higher profits, thus creating more dollars to invest, more demand for workers, in the virtuous cycle of capitalism.

Those who view tariffs through the perspective of production --- believing we must produce most of what we consume, to maintain the incomes of our people who work in manufacturing, while retaining the knowledge of industrial traditions that made us an economic superpower --- are more inclined to favor tariffs to balance our trade, especially with countries that erect barriers to keep our products out of their markets. They say that any money saved by importing more than we produce only increases consumption by requiring more government debt to relieve Americans whose wages are decaying and jobs vanishing because of imports.

We might make the Free Trade vs. Tariffs closing arguments:

The Case for Free Trade.

1. Free Trade is one of our founding principles. We are a revolutionary, anti-colonial, anti-imperialist country. We want the world open to competitive trade where we can sell to other countries and buy from them without either our

government or theirs interfering with business decisions on where to produce the goods and services traded.

2. Free trade, when practiced reciprocally, is the engine of efficiency, providing consumers with the best products at the lowest possible prices. Foreign competition replaces industries where we have no competitive efficiency advantage. It forces us to turn away from dying industries and focus our resources on newer and higher value industries where the future growth is, thereby promoting economic growth and higher wages.

3. Free Trade constrains the ability of our government to impose unbearable taxes and regulations on individuals and businesses. With free trade, our businesses have the option of packing off to another country to produce goods and services we consume.

4. Countries that trade together do not make war on their customers in other countries.

5. It doesn't matter whether other countries reciprocate our open market. If they're too "stupid" to buy our products, it doesn't mean we should be stupid by refusing to buy theirs.

Case for tariffs

1. Tariffs are also a founding principle. Alexander Hamilton wrote: *Not only the wealth, but the independence and security of a country, appear to be materially connected with the prosperity of manufactures. Every nation, with a view to those great objects, ought to endeavor to possess within itself all the essentials of national supply.* President George Washington sided with his view.

2. Adam Smith, the father of free trade, recognized that manufacturing employment is essential to economic and social stability, and perhaps should not be handed off to low-wage countries. Manufacturing creates supply chains below it and distribution chains above it in a way no other sector of the economy does. *The most opulent nations, indeed, generally excel all their neighbors in agriculture as well as in manufactures; but they are commonly more distinguished by their superiority in the latter than in the former.*

3. Free trade with low-wage countries does not necessarily promote efficiency. It may encourage American companies to forego investing in improved business processes and automation if they can reduce the cost of labor by moving production overseas.

4. Free trade may destroy vibrant industries. Most new industries are spawned from existing industries. If existing industries are offshored, new ones cannot evolve from the departed. Even when a new industry is invented in the United States, it may not remain unless protected by tariffs. It did not take China long to surpass us as the leading producer of solar panels and batteries for electric vehicles.

5. Tariffs may revitalize industries, increase competition, and lower prices to consumers by inducing new American startups to enter the industry or foreign companies to relocate production here. Friends of tariffs say that resulted from Reagan's and Trump's tariffs.

6. We must ask if it is fair to allow foreign companies that produce in other countries to extract profits tax-free from the United States when companies producing in the United

States are taxed on their profits and their workers are taxed on their wages.

7. If free trade promotes economic growth, why did growth stagnate *after* NAFTA and GATT, and fall into the Great Depression of 2008-2015?

8. The trade deficit is also a GDP, employment, debt, tax, and skills deficit. Every industry that goes overseas is a permanent subtraction from our GDP. Without tariffs, the trade deficit escalates, because the more we ship our economy overseas, the less we make sell to other countries. As the trade deficit increases, so does the national debt, because without producing goods and services, we have nothing to trade, other than inflationary fiat dollars, to trade for what we require from abroad.

After weighing these arguments, my recommended trade policies are:

*   Acknowledge that bilateral trade with kindred countries like Canada, Australia and the UK are mutually beneficial common markets where trade is balanced, as is our trade with 18 of the countries we have free trade agreements with, and most countries we have GATT trade with. Where the trade is balanced, tariffs, if imposed at all, should be for revenue generation, the way other countries impose VAT taxes on our exports, and not for protectionism.

*   Understand that poor countries may be purposed by our multinational corporations as labor substitution markets to replace Americans with foreign workers, not common markets to buy our exports. Labor substitution countries

may need to be tariffed to protect our workers and our tax revenues.

- Understand that trade with blocs like the European Union may be detrimental because they protect their trade with each other by placing barriers to trade with us, and tariffs may be our only answer to balance the trade.

- Understand that multilateral trade agreements like the Trans-Pacific Partnership are composed of countries with a common interest in accessing our market while imposing trade barriers against our exports. Nothing can be gained in a trading bloc that can't be gained by bilateral agreements simpler to monitor and enforce.

- Impose tariffs only on trade with countries that inflict perennial chronic trade deficits on us. Make the first round of tariffs equivalent to the VATs they charge on our exports. If, after one year, the trade is still unbalanced against us, then make the tariffs proportional to the trade imbalance ratio. If China's trade advantage is selling 3 to 1 to us, then their tariff needs to be 200%. If Japan's advantage is 2 to 1, they need a tariff of 200%. If the European Union's ratio is 1.5, they need a tariff of 50%, and so on.

We should view this question as more than the economics of cost increases tariffs may (or may not) impose on consumers. There is social and economic value in keeping our people employed making the products sold in this country, and knowledge value maintaining industrial traditions. Knowledge handed off to other countries can never be recovered. In considering circumstances where tariffs may be justly applied, we are thinking of the economic future of our descendants as well as ourselves.

Other Books by Alan Sewell

http://www.amazon.com/Alan-Sewell/e/B00557PQDY

If you liked this this book, here are others of political and economic interest, explains the economic history of the country, including the larger history wrapped around tariffs.

The Diary of American Exceptionalism: Pivotal Events in American History 1783 - 2025 Kindle Edition
by Alan Sewell (Author) | Format: Kindle Edition
4.1 ★★★★☆ ∨ 44 ratings   3.9 on Goodreads 24 ratings   See all formats and editions

"If we could first know where we are, and whither we are tending, we could better judge what to do, and how to do it."

So said Abraham Lincoln as he contemplated the great issues of containing slavery and preserving the Union. Now, after another era of turbulent political chaos, including repudiation of traditional American values by many elites in politics and academia, we are embarked on a GREAT RESTORATION of respect for our Founding principles.

This book is written to show where we are, and whither we are tending, by explaining our current political controversies in context of where we have been at similar crisis points in the past:

Fragmentation --- Federalism --- Union (1783-1815)
Secession --- War --- Nationalism (1858-1867)
Wealth --- Depression --- Empire (1890-1900)
Wealth --- Depression --- Liberalism (1929-1934)
Chaos --- Humiliation --- Conservatism (1968-1980)
The Great Recession to the Great Restoration (Contemporary)

It is written as a distilled essence of American history, explained in the words of the people who lived it. It focuses narrowly but intensively on cycles of quantum change that channeled us into new political and economic directions. Now that the recent election has embarked us upon another turning point in our history, it may provide insights into our future direction by shining it through the prism of our past.

https://www.amazon.com/Diary-American-Exceptionalism-Alan-Sewell-ebook/dp/B01H2HGCNC

The Diary of American Exceptionalism: Pivotal Events in American History 1783 - 2025 Kindle Edition

If we could first know where we are, and whither we are tending, we could better judge what to do, and how to do it."

So said Abraham Lincoln as he contemplated the great issues of containing slavery and preserving the Union. Now, after another era of turbulent political chaos, including repudiation of traditional American values by many elites in politics and academia, we are embarked on a GREAT RESTORATION of respect for our Founding principles.

This book is written to show where we are, and whither we are tending, by explaining our current political controversies in context of where we have been at similar crisis points in the past:

Fragmentation — Federalism — Union (1783-1815)
Secession — War — Nationalism (1858-1867)
Wealth — Depression — Empire (1890-1900)
Wealth — Depression — Liberalism (1929-1934)
Chaos — Humiliation — Conservatism (1968-1980)
The Great Recession to the Great Restoration (Contemporary)

It is written as a distilled essence of American history, explained in the words of the people who lived it. It focuses narrowly but intensively on cycles of quantum change that channeled us into new political and economic directions. Now that the recent election has embarked us upon another turning point in our history, it may provide insights into our future direction by shining it through the prism of our past. The historical context of tariffs was derived from this book.

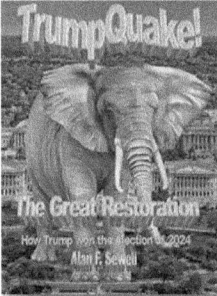

Trumpquake: The Great Restoration: How Trump won the election of 2024 Kindle Edition

by Alan Sewell (Author)   Format: Kindle Edition

4.2 ★★★★☆   3 ratings   See all formats and ed

The current and historical perspective of how Trump won the election of 2024 and turned The Great Reset into The Gr Restoration.

Print Length	Language	Publication date	File size	Page Flip
255 pages	English	November 5, 2024	8189 KB	Enabled

See all details

Report an issue with this product or seller

https://www.amazon.com/Trumpquake-Great-Restoration-Trump-election-ebook/dp/B0D9TXX3FG

Trumpquake: The Great Restoration: How Trump won the election of 2024 Kindle Edition

The current and historical perspective of how Trump won the election of 2024 and turned The Great Reset into The Great Restoration.

TrumpQuake! explains the political and economic issues that enabled Donald Trump to prevail in the 2024 election despite a thousand faults and blunders in his first term. It places the election in historical context with prior elections.

About the Author

"Understanding history is a key to understanding the present and extrapolating the future."

- Alan Sewell

I've lived and worked in the United States, Canada, Latin America, and Asia, having made a career of developing trading systems for multinational corporations. I thus bring a practical, as well as historical, perspective to the discussion of tariffs.

I became a student of history while young, publishing my first nationally prominent political and historical magazine articles in 1981. Since then, I have written articles and books on many aspects of American history, politics, and economics. My insights of how history illuminates current events are popular in *The Wall Street Journal* and in book reviews, receiving kudos from Republicans, Democrats, and Independents:

- This book and Alan Sewell's review are so insightful as to what needs to be done to save the economy ...Why don't we have a presidential candidate with the author's or Alan Sewell's comprehension of the economic problems?

- Alan, I agree and want to thank you, personally, as well. I thank you for your remarkable commentary supported by hard facts. You have changed my mind about some things through the excellence of your arguments, always supported by hard facts and documentation. You are an asset beyond compare to this community. Thank you so very much.

- Mr. Sewell has made me rethink a number of ideas I thought were set in historical concrete.

- I only wish the country's "leaders" who fight endlessly in Congress to prevent the other side from making any progress would read this concise and well-reasoned review. It is better than reading a whole book about economics and succinctly states many ideas I have long held since I studied economics and then studied people. Excellent review and analysis that goes beyond the book.

- Your advice could not have been more eloquently phrased had Winston Churchill been your editor.

- Great Review! I do so agree with every word in your review. I'll be reviewing, reading your books. Ever consider running for President?

- This is a great, thoughtful review. It's refreshing to hear from a someone who really does have an open mind.

- BEST REVIEW on this entire topic I ever read!!! Your willingness to share it with the rest of us - as the topic relates to a particular historical work - is much appreciated. Thank you.

- Once again, thank you, Alan Sewell. You are one of the most insightful and rational Americans in existence.

- Alan, your comments restored my faith that our nation can become less divisive if people were able to listen with an open mind to a well-reasoned discussion of an important topic. On the other hand, I am very concerned that few people who share your leanings are as open as you are to listen to a reasonable discussion.

- I just discovered this review and, from there, found your others. These are some of the most thoughtful comments I have found and are worth reading for reasons well beyond book reviews. Thank you.

I've devoted my life to analyzing historical and current events and applying their historical lessons to today's business and economic issues.

Although every day is a new day, the new days are layered on top of repeating cycles of history as old as Mankind. The more we understand the cycles of history, the more complete our understanding of the present will be.

Feedback

Please address feedback to alsnewideas@gmail.com